Birds for all Seasons

Chronicles from the Thames Valley

Birds for all Seasons

Chronicles from the Thames Valley

by

JAMES MONK

Illustrated by
Robert Gillmor

PICA PRESS
SUSSEX

© 1997 James Monk and Robert Gillmor

Pica Press
(an imprint of Helm Information Ltd),
The Banks, Mountfield,
Nr. Robertsbridge,
East Sussex TN32 5JY

ISBN 1-873403-64-X

A CIP catalogue record for this book is available from the British Library.

07637316

Production and design by Fluke Art, Bexhill-on-Sea, E Sussex
Printed by Penna Press, St Albans, Hertfordshire

Contents

*"The world is a strange place
and the strangest thing of all is that we are here to discuss it."*

Preface

These short chronicles have been modified and enlarged from their original appearance in the *Goring Gap News*, an award-winning monthly village publication from the Thames Valley. I am very grateful to the magazine's proprietors for permission to use that material for this slim volume.

John Elgood and Dr Derrick Foskett both very carefully read an earlier version of the text and kindly pointed out several mistakes. In particular I wish to thank Dr David Snow for his meticulous attention to the text, including one or two useful alterations and several pleasing embellishments, including the title of the book. I must, of course, be given the blame for any remaining omissions and errors.

Robert Gillmor, despite his crowded calender, very kindly undertook to provide his ever charming drawings, which so enhance the text. He also executed the handsome painting of the Red Kites which appears on the jacket. The original painting was a retirement present to Professor Curnow of Reading University and I am extremely grateful to him for so generously allowing a reproduction to be used to enhance the appearance of this book. I am very indebted to and wish to thank Christopher Helm for his scholarly editing and more particularly for providing some enriching quotations from his wide acquaintance with the classics and English Literature. The text would be that much poorer without their contributions.

It was a pleasure for me to compose these short essays because I was able to divest myself of the strict discipline involved in the editing for some 30 years of scientific journals and other publications of learned ornithological societies and to allow myself the indulgence of relaxing into anthropomorphic sentiment. To describe at times the behaviour of birds as if their emotions and reactions were the same as ours can be forgiven if it is not over-serious, but does, at the same time, evoke a recollection which illustrates a bird's particular characteristic. I have enjoyed doing so, and I hope that others may take pleasure from it as well. Birds are there to be a delight, full of character, some with unusual habits, some dull, some handsome, others beautiful, some of them villainous, but all of them able momentarily at least to draw admiration for one attribute or another.

Goring-on-Thames   *James Monk*
August 1997

The Red Kite

T IS very seldom that one has a new bird to look for in the skies over the Goring Gap in South Oxfordshire, but the Red Kite *Milvus milvus* has been exciting a lot of interest there recently. Until eight years ago it had only been recorded in Oxfordshire twice this century. Today, happily, though anything but common, it may well be seen in south Oxfordshire and over the Chilterns on any day in the year. It is an impressive bird of prey. Rusty coloured above, it has a conspicuously forked chestnut tail, long wings, angled when it soars, showing a pale patch on the underside at the base of the black flight feathers and a streaky whitish head. About the same size as a Buzzard, the Kite's wings are more pointed, neither so broad nor blunt-ended as the Buzzard's, and its flight is much more buoyant. Like the Buzzard it has a plaintive mewing call, sometimes almost a whistle.

Until the last 150 years, this grand bird was common all over Britain, and had probably been so for a millennium or more. Certainly in the 15th and 16th centuries it was numerous in all the big cities of England, its invaluable scavenging habits giving it protection — you could, indeed, be fined for killing one.

Turner, the son of a mere tanner, published in 1544 an important work, *"De Historia Avium — a short and succinct history of the principal birds noticed by Pliny and Aristotle"*, effusively dedicated to Edward, Prince of Wales, son and heir of Henry VIII. The Latin milvus he states "in English [is] a glede [glider], a puttok, a kyte...." and quotes Pliny (A.D.23-79) : "They seem ... to have taught mankind the art of steering, by the turning of the tail, nature thus shewing in the sky what might be useful in the sea. Milvi lie hidden in the winter months, yet not until Hirundines depart. They are reported also to be affected with the gout about the solstice." Turner himself remarks that the Kite "..in England is abundant and remarkably rapacious". Elsewhere he writes : "Our birds are much larger than the German birds ... and much greedier. For such is the audacity of our Kites, that they dare to snatch bread from children, fish from women, and handkerchiefs from off hedges, and out of men's hands. They are accustomed to carry off caps from off men's heads when they are building their nests." It would have been unlike Shakespeare not to have made reference to one of this familiar bird's less welcome traits: "When the kite builds, look to lesser linen." Rags may still commonly be found in the lining of Kites' nests.

An illustration in a 15th century medical treatise shows a Kite standing on a man's head, "plain testimony to the tameness of these privileged city cleaners" as an early 20th century author remarks. Scavenging is the usual mode of feeding for all 'milvi', and in the hideously unhygienic days of streets filthy with sewage and worse, the Kite's usefulness in ridding the gutters and yards of their nauseating rotting garbage and carrion was to be greatly encouraged.

These habits, more appreciated than resented, became unwelcome when sewage disposal gradually became effective, so that well before the end of the Victorian era the Kite had been exterminated from Britain except for a tiny relict population in a corner of Wales. There, all this century until recently, despite persistent persecution by keepers and egg collectors, the Kite clung on to its status as a breeding British bird, the numbers remaining at a precarious 3-12 pairs from year to year. There was no population dispersal and badly needed recruits were not forthcoming. This situation somehow changed, because in 1954 there was an increase to 15 pairs and some 55 birds. In 1961 a young bird ringed in Wales was picked up dead under overhead wires at Woodstock in Oxfordshire. By 1972 the population had increased to about 19-26 pairs and 80 individuals. In 1972 too a German ringed bird was recovered in the area.

The improvement was certainly also helped by better wardening of the critical oak wood habitats of the breeding sites; and the picture in Wales today is happily much more satisfactory and stable thanks to greater insight into the birds' needs and care from the Royal Society for the Protection of Birds.

In Berkshire, as in Oxfordshire, the Kite was rarely seen, with only one or two records this century before 1970; but since then, rather surprisingly, there may be 3-4 sightings per year. However, in Oxfordshire and over the Chilterns the picture has recently been transformed. English Nature and the RSPB have been introducing numbers of free-flying young adult Kites into Oxfordshire since 1989, and by now, breeding is regular all over the area. In 1996 the RSPB monitored all the breeding pairs and reported 33 nests in "southern England" (mostly around south Oxfordshire), rearing as many as 80 free-flying young successfully. This remarkable achievement has been brought about by cooperation between enlightened landowners and keepers and the conservation bodies. Even so, 5-6 Kites have been found poisoned, just going to prove that some unprincipled and contemptible self-serving individuals flout the law and decency at will. Nevertheless to all others, the introductions provide a most pleasing addition to Oxfordshire skies. With the present greater interest and understanding about this elegant and handsome bird, it seems certain that the Red Kite will be seen regularly over the Thames Valley into the next millennium and beyond. Look to your lesser linen!

Birds in January

Nutcracker *Nucifraga caryocatactes*

O Winter, ruler of the inverted year!

William Cowper, *The Winter Evening.*

N JANUARY, cold and food shortage can be disastrous for birds; it is the worst and most calamitous month of their winter. Severe frosts may not be too dire provided they last no more than 2-3 days. Frost kills off much of the insect life so essential in the diet of many birds, or compels other prey to become torpid and therefore inactive; stationary objects are not seen so readily by birds. With ice forming over water puddles and bird baths, lack of drinking water is another ill of winter. Some birds take in all the water they require from their food, but this is a specialised adaptation not usual in our garden birds; so it is considerate to top up the water in the bird bath continually through all frosty weather. It is surprising too to find that on the exceptional day of sunshine in January birds will often come to bathe, though the water may be little above freezing.

Many species of birds have a habit of storing food in hard times, and even ahead of hard times. The Nutcracker, of northern Europe, is a largeish white-speckled brown bird, a member of the crow family, with a large, heavy-looking beak which is adapted for extracting the kernels from nuts and fir-cones. One individual has been known to package 15-20 hazel nuts together into its throat pouch and bury them individually in the ground in different places. Thereafter it was watched, weeks later, retrieving the nuts successfully on 4 out of 5 attempts, even when the ground's surface appearance had been quite altered by a heavy snowfall. Another example is the Acorn Woodpecker of California and the SW states of the USA, which works in groups, co-operatively storing large numbers of acorns in purposely made holes in tree trunks, larders which they defend tenaciously. Tits will even store insects if they are lucky enough to find a large collection of them hiding in shelter from very cold weather, but they probably eat them within a few hours. Rooks regularly, and Jackdaws sometimes, store a variety of foods, and the handsome black, white and red Great Spotted Woodpeckers frequently store fir-cones.

A life saving feature in hard weather is the fluffing out of their body feathers by birds, producing the more chubby rounded appearance of Robins, in life as well as on Christmas cards. The bird is in essence wrapping itself in a duvet made of down. Projecting from the shaft at the base of each body feather there is a collection of soft 'plumules', similar to those on the down feathers which the Eider Duck plucks from its breast to line the nest and cover its eggs. Early this century the down of these birds breeding in large colonies in Scotland and elsewhere was harvested, in amounts sufficient to provide down for pillows, and the practice continues even today for the most expensive duvets. To prevent loss of body heat, all a bird's feathers except the wings and tail can be erected, that is, made to fluff out much more than normal, making the downy base to the feathers more erect. This produces a very effective duvet, which traps and above all retains the heat given off from the skin, thus helping to prevent the bird from being frozen. In our own homes huddling oneself close in even quite a thin, light duvet as a shawl or body wrap is highly recommended for the aged and immobile in severely cold spells.

These safeguards are alone not enough security for a bird at night in a cold and unfriendly environment — a safe roost is an important requirement, one that will provide protection against both cold and predators. For many small birds a tree hole is an obvious haven, comparatively safe from marauders and a place where its body heat is retained by the confines of the hole. A hole nest-site is usually used in the summer for roosting in by at least one of a pair until the young get too large, and old nests and tree holes are often used in winter. Huddling together of several birds adds to the warmth of the shelter — sometimes Treecreepers have been found in bunches of ten or more in a communal roost, all with their heads in and their tails sticking out; whereas a dozen Long-tailed Tits may be found in a long line on a horizontal branch, pressed close together.

Quite a different type of group roosting is indulged in by Quail; they will sometimes form a small circle in a sheltered piece of ground, all of them facing outwards, like sentries round a camp! Game birds like Grouse and Ptarmigan, which live on moorland, will burrow under the winter snow into the heather, forming tunnels and chambers in which they can keep quite warm, protected from winds and frost. Waders will huddle in flocks on wide open mudflats, the smaller waders often taking advantage of their larger cousins to use them as wind-breaks. Spectacular roosts are often formed by Starlings, sometimes of tens of thousands of birds; while the Quelea, a small weaver-bird of Africa, has been counted in millions very often, both at roosts and in breeding colonies. So great are its numbers at times that it is a serious pest, stripping entire acreages of seed crops in a matter of hours, as swiftly as a plague of locusts.

Slightly surprisingly the Pied (or Willie) Wagtail, which is anything but a sociable bird at other times, preferring to live and feed singly, is a communal rooster, most commonly in reedbeds, but also in trees, and even in greenhouses. There is a tree on the forecourt of Reading railway station that may accommodate up to 100 wagtails twittering or sleeping in it overnight, quite unperturbed by the lights or by the traffic and pedestrians passing unawares at all hours of darkness close to and under the tree.

The Barn Owl

It was the owl that shrieked, the fatal bellman,
which gives the stern'st good-night

William Shakespeare, *Macbeth*.

HE BARN OWL *Tyto alba* is found all over the world, across Europe, Africa, Asia, India, Indonesia, in the Pacific, Australia and both the Americas; and is absent only from the icy northern parts of Central Asia and Siberia. Also known as the White Owl, it is the Screech Owl of many countries, distinguishing it from the Tawny or Brown Owl, which familiarly hoots *Tu wit tu woooo*. The Barn Owl's loud, daunting, gruesome screech is generally heard only at night; in the day a rather intimidating hissing is more usual, as well as grunts and snores.

Like nearly all owls, the Barn Owl will breed readily in captivity, but it needs expert care and plenty of room in which to fly. Captive bred birds can then be released into suitable habitat to supplement the sadly diminishing natural population. Also, like many other hole-nesting species, it will make good use of nest boxes and the farmer who puts them up in his grain filled barns and old buildings — the more the better — gains much from a good riddance to unwanted rodents, free.

The Barn Owl has beautiful, soft plumage, entirely white on the breast and underparts (though there is an uncommon dark-breasted form), while the back and the upperside of the wings are a golden-buff and dove-grey, with an intricate patterning of spots and patches on the feathers. The softness is due to special feathering. There is an extra velcro-like arrangement binding the individual feathers to each other, so that there is no rustling of the wings when the bird is hunting. Flight is quite silent. The plumage is compact and dense, cloaking the comparatively small body. The bird's light weight in relation to its large wings gives it a buoyant look as it glides or slowly flaps while patrolling over its feeding meadow in the twilight.

A characteristic of almost all owls is the large head and the broad flat face. The Barn Owl's head is particularly large, with a cowl-shaped crown and a placid appealing face. The flat face means that both eyes of an owl face directly forward, giving excellent two-eyed vision, with the enormous advantage this brings of being able to judge distances accurately, for example when pouncing from the air on an unsuspecting vole. The huge eyes are also another important modification — they let in extra quantities of light, since much of the Barn Owl's hunting is done in twilight. It is, however, not true that owls can see in darkness, nor is infra-red light any help to them. They are exceptional in being able to blink, and even wink, with their upper lid. On the other hand, owls' eyes can barely move in their sockets, a handicap which has been overcome by yet another adaptation enabling them to rotate their necks through at least 180°, some species reputedly through 270°. Thus they can inspect what is immediately behind them without moving any other part of their body or feet.

It is a ghostly creature, the Barn Owl, and the fact that it likes to nest in old buildings such as church belfries, means that it is not uncommonly seen in cemeteries. In consequence it has attracted many local superstitions and myths, particularly the reputation that it is a messenger of death or evil, Shakespeare's "fatal bellman". In Borneo, a timely shriek from the Barn Owl will oblige a party on the war path immediately to return home lest illness or worse befall. Equally prophetically, in the south of France a shriek from the chimney of a house in which a child was being born, it was believed, indicated that it would be a girl; but it is not recorded how often the owl got it right.

It is a pleasure to believe that owls are ever wise. A branch of the owl family, of which the Little Owl is one, has been given the scientific name *Athene*, after the Goddess of Wisdom. The most charming of this group, according to T.H.White, was Archimedes, the fellow that Merlin carried about on his shoulder and who often had to calm down the old magician when he had lost his temper because he had got his spells in a twist. Would that we all had such a familiar to keep us in our place.

Owls have also developed a very keen sense of hearing to help them live their twilight life. Their ears, which have nothing to do with those tufted feathers protruding from the top of the heads of so-called 'eared owls', are much larger than those of birds which go to bed at dusk and hope to sleep all night. Also, in some owl species the ear-holes are not arranged symmetrically, allowing the bird to pin-point sounds even more exactly. So very sensitive is their hearing, that they have been observed catching prey, such as field mice, in total darkness, guiding themselves silently onto their unsuspecting victim purely by the tiny sounds made as it feeds.

The Barn Owl is a marvellous example of the many and important adaptations that have evolved to help it pursue a mode of life that over the years had not been exploited by other species. What a success it has made of it! It is gruesome to think that after millions of years it is only selfish Man who is still thoughtlessly and severely persecuting this enchanting and specially endowed bird. But there is hope. In England at least, thanks to the efforts of the conservation bodies, we have come to recognise the wonderful natural history and aesthetic beauty of these beneficial creatures. In Malaysia, Barn Owls are being encouraged to breed in oil-palm planta-tions in order to keep the rats under control. Perhaps after thousands of years of superstitious persecution, the light is beginning to shine through.

The Jackdaw

Good faith, I am no wiser than a daw

William Shakespeare, *Henry VI Part II*.

HE JACKDAW *Corvus monedula*, is one of Nature's enjoyable rogues – they cry "Jack" so cheerily and mill about in small or large bunches, appearing nearly always to be in a party mood. But they are not much loved by their smaller brethren, whose offspring they are quite happy to molest and devour.

One of the black crows, smaller than the Carrion Crow and the Rook, the Jackdaw's whole plumage is black except the grey nape and sides of head and neck, which distinguishes it from all the others. It has a beady, pearl-grey or white, inquisitively extrovert eye. One would never trust an acquaintance with a sharp look like the Jackdaw's.

This charismatic bird was intensively studied by Professor Konrad Lorenz of Austria, who shared the 1973 Nobel Prize in Medicine with Dr Niko Tinbergen, eminent in research of great distinction in the Department of Zoological Field Studies at Oxford. The award was perceptive and important. These two scientists were the pioneers of ethology, the study of behaviour, a subject barely acknowledged in the 1940s and '50s when they were doing their research and little recognised at that time in the field of human psychology and medicine. But their work inspired many scientists into using similar methods for investigating animal behaviour, notably that of the great apes, and inevitably of man, which led to new insights into the behaviour of the human child and its parents in illness and various other situations. It re-emphasised the need for acute and detailed observation of behaviour. Tinbergen's work was mostly with gulls, at first with Herring Gulls and later with Black-headed Gulls, and these studies together with those of the Jackdaw by Lorenz, opened the eyes of the scientific world to these biologists' innovative theories.

A pert, mischievous alertness is conspicuous in the Jackdaw, especially as it struts across a lawn or field with a jaunty walking gait, dapper and confident. At times it may get extraordinarily excited, particularly with a crowd of others, performing frenzied aerobatics for minutes on end, without explanation (unless it is just youthful vigour?), diving headlong at a companion, side-slipping and flipping over onto its back, swooping heavenwards again, shouting the while apparently for the pure joy of living.

Nothing if not social, the Jackdaw prefers a nest site fairly close to others, as in a spread of chimneys in a group of houses; but it also nests in holes in trees and, in wilder country, in ruins and cliff holes and even in rabbit burrows. Dead sticks are used for the foundations of its nest, and since it will resort to its summer villa year after year, and will always add to the nest material, the accumulation of sticks can become massive and cause fumes (and fuming) if this happens in a chimney that is in use and the obstruction discovered only when the first fire of autumn is lit.

Jackdaws pair for life, though widows and widowers will mate again. Their mutual affection is shown in the spring by the male bringing and presenting many morsels of food to his mate; and she shows her devotion by cleaning and nibbling his long silken neck feathers, to his evident enjoyment. The male's main gesture in courtship display is to bow repeatedly, sometimes raising his crown feathers while pressing his beak into his chest, thus showing off his handsome grey hood. The displays of most birds are related to making prominent some feature of their plumage by gesture or posture, whether in courtship or defence or aggression, or any other predicament. They provide visual communication, "signals for survival", as Tinbergen called it, which if ignored may lead to losing a mate, or to a brawl or even worse.

The same is to be seen in nearly all animals — the dog and the horse, for example, make obvious signals by moving their ears, while posture and movements of limbs in man, known popularly today as 'body language', convey equally recognisable states of mind.

Though there is some movement of Jackdaws into Britain in autumn from Scandinavia, the population of the British Isles is sedentary, and pairs can often be seen in winter visiting their nest sites. They are, however, very gregarious and outside the breeding season spend most of their time in flocks, congregating with Rooks, feeding in the fields on grain or on grubs, beetles and worms, often looking for these in cowpats, which can be seen to be pitted with many beak holes or scattered all about. It is interesting that often on hillsides or chalk downs where such parties come to feed, one may come across halves of empty walnut shells where no walnut trees exist. Are they perhaps brought there by Jackdaws and Rooks? If not by whom?

In autumn and winter, mixed flocks, in which Jackdaws are outnumbered by Rooks, can be seen towards dusk flying high over the Thames in the Goring Gap, drifting, or if it is getting late flying determinedly, towards and over the top of Streatley Hill and beyond to woods this side of Hampstead Norreys, where they roost, several hundred or a thousand birds together. These have commingled from different daytime haunts, pausing on their evening journey at regularly visited localities, finally settling in a field close to the roost, the whole gathering full of continuous noise, "jacks", "caws" and the many other raucous sounds with which these birds communicate. But suddenly, when it is nearly dark, the whole mob rises together, hurtling into the trees in a noisy rush, and within perhaps less than two minutes everyone is settled and a complete silence has descended. What a dramatic way of going to bed!

⊰ Birds in February ⊱

Long-eared Owl *Asio otus*

So, while the light fails
On a winter's afternoon, in a secluded chapel
History is now and England

T.S. Eliot, *Four Quartets*.

EBRUARY brings occasional encouraging signs for the optimist that winter is passing. By the end of the month Rooks will be seen attending to the old nests that have not been destroyed by the winter storms, as like as not 'borrowing' twigs from nests other than their own. Their noisy, enjoyable conversations may be heard on any bright, cold sunny day, but their deep wool-lined nests will not hold eggs until quite late next month. Herons start building even earlier, but their tree nests, in contrast to the Rooks', are huge platforms of twigs, usually with little or no cup, at risk from strong winds and clumsy landings that will tip the delicately blue eggs over the nest edge. The Rook's nest seems far better designed, deep enough to prevent the wildest swaying of the tree branches from depositing the eggs on the ground.

An early nester, now regrettably much rarer everywhere, including on the Berkshire Downs and the Ridgeway, is the Long-eared Owl, of which more than two pairs used to nest, and may still do so, annually on the downs at the edges of the Fair Mile. They use old nests of Crows, Rooks, Magpies and squirrels' drays in which to lay their 4-5 eggs. Great big birds with bright yellow saucer eyes, they always look wise and friendly. Their 'ears' have nothing to do with hearing; they are merely elongated feathers which jut up from the sides of their crowns and which they can erect or lower in tune with their temper.

The Mistle Thrush, appropriately called by country folk the Stormcock, will have started to shout from the tree tops by the end of the month. It gets its common name from its fancy for mistletoe berries, and it used to be called "Mizzy Dick" in Northumberland. Its harsh alarm notes gained it the name of Jercock or Chercock in some counties and in Antrim, in Ireland, it was once known as Corney Keevor. Extraordinarily, in some parts of France it used to be given the credit for speaking seven languages, something the average Britisher would never have considered possible for himself, let alone a bird. There seems little doubt that 'Mistle' is the correct spelling rather than 'Missel', since its liking for mistletoe berries was a fact known even to Aristotle, and this habit gives rise to its Latin name *viscivorus*. The ancients believed that the berries only became fertile after they had passed through the gut of a Mistle Thrush. Whether this is so or not, the spread of mistletoe from tree to tree is certainly at least partly the result of their transportation by Mistle Thrushes.

Bird table frequenters in February will continue to enjoy man's largesse in the garden and happily the Robin will begin to change its song from its winter stanzas to its tinkling springtime song.

Little other proper song is heard at this time, and despite fleeting signs of promise, February is rather dull for birds, an inclement month, with little to recommend it, except perhaps that it has 2-3 fewer days of winter than its companions. It has, of course, long since lost its leap year relationship with female matrimonial proposals, a tradition comprehensively dismissed as an anachronism by the militant half of our unisex society. Oh pusillanimous men!

One year is like any other for our birds. In nearly all of those species in which the males and females look identical, such as the Robin, and in which the male holds and defends a territory, problems arise when a female casually intrudes, naturally to the fury of the undiscerning male. He, wretched lad, finds that his bravado is completely ignored and the intruder continues to treat the territory as her own. It may take the poor boy several days for him to recognise that he is making a fool of himself and to realise that this is the companion he has been so ardently singing for. As like as not another male may then enter from without and dispute with him over his newly recognised mate. But in a bird's world most antagonism is displayed in posture and by aggressive gestures rather than in attack, and the intruder, with his guilty conscience, retreats before the landowner without fight — but only as far as a shared border. However, if this mutual boundary is then in turn transgressed by the neighbouring landowner, the roles are quickly reversed. Blackbirds exemplify these demarcation disputes, footing it back and forth for many days in succession until the boundaries are accepted by both sides. Would that our domestic, national and international disputes were settled so simply.

The Black-headed Gull

Whish! A gull. Gulls. Far calls

James Joyce, *Finnegans Wake*.

HE BLACK-HEADED GULL *Larus ridibundus* has no black on its head at all. The colour is a rich chocolate brown, only present in the spring and summer, its trim appearance emphasised by a white ring round the bird's eye. After the autumn moult, all that remains is a dark smudge on the side of the head. In flight there is a conspicuous and distinguishing pure white leading edge to the wing. At the end of a dreary long winter it is a cheerful delight suddenly to recognise that this dapper gull is newly attired in its breeding headgear — a smart, well cut, shiny, backless chocolate balaclava. To see it thus sitting on the warning notice "Danger" guarding Goring weir, is to know that Spring is imminent.

As everyone knows, there are seagulls and BBCgulls. The BBC's gull is a Herring Gull, shouting its head off in the background of some coastal or island scene. They, and Black-headed Gulls, can often be seen winging an erratic way through the Goring Gap in the Thames Valley, usually towards evening in the autumn and winter, journeying perhaps to the Theale gravel pits on the Kennet, or even to the far off big London reservoirs not far from Heathrow airport, to roost after a day's feeding in pastures new.

Birds for all Seasons

The Black-headed Gull is one of a large group of smaller gulls. It does not spend most of its life scouring the oceans like some gulls; nor is it confined to the coast, being found inland at any time of year, easily the commonest gull to be seen away from the sea. It is not a fisherman, but eats mainly animal material, especially insects and earthworms. But it is also a very determined scavenger on land and water and will voraciously consume almost any household waste. Squabbling over some morsel of garbage is a common sight. Its greed, or appetite, sometimes calls for spectacular aerobatic skills. In St James's Park in London, small flocks gather, often milling in strident competition and with astonishing deftness to catch food flung by visitors from the bridge that crosses the Lake — it is quite a pastime for both parties at the feast. Black-headed Gulls will congregate anywhere where people distribute scraps, such as below Goring-on-Thames bridge, where the ducks also grow fat. Indeed, to watch their startling agility in catching high tossed crusts of bread is joyously rewarding.

Nesting is on the ground in colonies, among sandhills, on shingle banks and small islands, in puddly marshes, at gravel pits, usually where there is live vegetation, often far inland. They sometimes number many hundreds of pairs and the noise created regales one from afar. So also can the 'pong'. William Turner, the father of English ornithology (c.1500-1568), in the 16th century described them appropriately as "always querulous and full of noise". Each pair lays 2-3 large eggs and in the past, big colonies on private land were much valued. One hundred and one years ago, Professor Alfred Newton, 1829-1907, one of the founders of the British Ornithologists' Union in 1859, wrote: "Some of the settlements of the Black-headed or 'Poewit' Gull . . .are a source of no small profit to their proprietors — the eggs, which are accounted a delicacy, being often taken on an orderly system up to a certain day, and the birds carefully protected" — an early example of enlightened and harmless exploitation. Such harvesting of the eggs of the colonially nesting gulls is pursued still on a small scale in many places in the British Isles to this day. The eggs were a welcome source of extra and very palatable food in Britain during the stringencies of the Second World War. In colonies of ground- and cliff-nesting birds, human disturbance rarely leads to desertion, and in an empty nest the hen bird will continue laying her eggs daily or on alternate days until allowed to keep the last two or three to give the comfort of a full clutch. Incubation normally starts after two eggs have been laid, giving the female plenty of time to fatten up well and rest. On Skokholm, for instance, the owner of the island, Ronald M. Lockley, a well known ornithologist and author, collected annually enough eggs of the Lesser Black-backed Gull to fill several 50 gallon barrels where they were preserved in the now out-dated preservative waterglass (sodium silicote in viscous solution) without any detriment to the colony. Sufficient nests are always carefully left unmolested when harvesting in order to allow the colony to continue to flourish. But an important requirement in the past was for as great a hatch of young as possible also to survive, for the fledglings, while still flightless, were corralled in netting enclosures, their destination the pot, after first having been fattened on a spanking good diet of liver and curds.

The Black-headed Gull is a welcome bird on farmland, devouring many pests. A familiar sight is a flock of these dapper gulls following the plough, settling on the overturned earth, searching for the disinterred insects and grubs, leap-frogging forward when the tractor gets too far away. Later, sated and full of leather-jackets and other pests, the birds will often move off and form a white carpet in the middle of a brown field while they rest and digest an excellent meal. The birds are safe and content, the farmer has benefited and anyone watching the gulls having their meal cannot fail to have been entertained. How eminently satisfactory!

The Magpie

One is sorrow, two is mirth
Three a wedding, four a birth

Traditional

 VILLAIN, plunderer, thief, murderer of other birds, cheeky — and rather beautiful. Thus the Magpie *Pica pica*, is described wherever it occurs — and that is over a vast area, from western Europe to Russia, Tibet, all Asia, China, and western Canada and the western USA. Like any creature with a wide range across the world, variation in colour and size occurs. All have the black and white plumage and the gorgeously long tail, graduated to a pointed tip in the shape of a flattened diamond. Our bird has a beautiful purple-blue gloss on the body becoming greenish on the tail.

The wing has a prominent white patch, and the belly and flanks are Persil white, contrasting with the rest of the plumage's iridescent black. Being a member of the crow family, it struts or hops about haughtily on its sturdy black legs and the beak is heavy and strong.

Plumage and size variations become readily recognisable across long geographical distances, changes that are termed a 'cline'. The Magpie has one geographical cline running down from northern Scandinavia to northwest Africa, the white patch on the wing getting smaller and smaller going south, as also does its size. In northwest Africa itself the bird has developed, rather inexplicably, a small bare patch of blue skin behind the eye. There is another cline running west to east, the wing becoming longer with more white on it towards the east, into Asia, and the iridescence gradually changing from blue to green. These changes, when well marked enough and thus easily recognisable, lead to the naming of 'subspecies', adding yet a third (subspecific) name to the generic and specific names (in that order). Thus our garden villain becomes *Pica pica pica*, while the Mongolian subspecies ends up as *Pica pica leucoptera* because of the extra white in its wing (*leucoptera* comes from the Classical Greek words meaning 'white-winged').

This system sounds very clumsy, but it is no clumsier than a surname followed by two Christian names to distinguish one individual from another. The scientific classification thus allows all ornithologists to speak unambiguously with one tongue about a single species and its subspecies. This trinomial system has an excellent pedigree, being an extension of Linnaeus's binomial system which he so brilliantly evolved in the middle of the 18th century and which has been in use now for 250 years.

Such a prominent bird as the Magpie has attracted myths in folklore, but the superstition in one place may be the opposite of that in another. Perhaps the most widespread of the Magpie superstitions is the raising of the hat in salutation when catching sight of one, to ward off bad luck. The Magpie, sometimes called Maggie, Marget, Magot-pie (Shakespeare), Pye Mag and other polite names, has been accused of many evils, including that of being a witch or sorcerer in disguise. It has been said to have seven of the devil's own hairs on its head and even of being satanic enough to desert its domed and thorn-protected nest if a cross is cut on the tree. By some accounts it refused to go inside Noah's ark, preferring to sit on the roof and jabber. Some myths inevitably involve medicinal beliefs, one of which states that drinking the broth in which it has been boiled will send the consumer crazy, while in contradiction another that the same broth will cure epilepsy. Take your choice, but why boil the poor bird in the first place? On the other hand the Magpie is given credit for some good habits, such as shrieking a warning at the imminent arrival of an unwanted visitor, but merely chattering if it is a friend. To have one perched on one's roof indicates that the house is safe from natural disasters; ominously, the Magpie is absent from coastal California. In Norway, the Magpie has always been considered a bird of good luck and was reported as long as 150 years ago to be approachable and fearless of man.

The lifestyle of the Magpie has changed considerably in England in the past 30 years. It is acquiring more nearly the character the Norwegians have given it, becoming a more suburban bird, profiting from domestic food scraps and bird tables and taking advantage of an absence of shotguns in semi-rural gardens. Hate him or love him, the Magpie will always be a cheerful and appealing sinner.

Birds in March

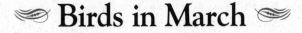

Great Crested Grebe *Podiceps cristatus*

Daffodils,
That come before the swallow dares, and take
The winds of March with beauty

William Shakespeare, *The Winter's Tale.*

I N MARCH, much of the oppressive greyness of winter is becoming less obtrusive and, despite the habitual gales, some of our resident birds have become cheeringly active.

Rooks have been repairing or building their nests since February, sometimes surreptitiously thieving twigs from their neighbours' nests, not always undetected and a brawl ensues. Elms used to be the favourite trees chosen for a rookery but since their devastation by Dutch Elm Disease, Rooks have adapted to many other and some much less tall species, apparently with little difficulty or harm befalling them. They will have eggs in their deep wool-lined nests by the end of March, the Carrion Crow, like the garden-marauding Magpie, not until early April.

The Chaffinch will have started singing at the end of last month. Their song is learned during their first year of life, but repertoires will change sometimes as the bird grows older, though separate local dialects and variations are slight and difficult to discern. Our Wren sings all the year, and will often burst into loud song if suddenly and unexpectedly disturbed, a rather pleasing reaction to fright. The Dunnock or Hedge Sparrow is another garden bird which can be heard singing in any month of the year, except during its autumn moult.

On rivers and lakes or gravel pits, Great Crested Grebes will have been building their floating, platform nests anchored under overhanging tree branches, but eggs are not often laid until next month. Pairs have been displaying to each other since February, face to face, breast to breast, very upright, heads and beaks wagging from side to side, enhancing their two small black crests and their large chestnut facial tippets. Their numbers have increased considerably, certainly so in the Goring Gap, over the last 20 years. Could this be due to fishermen returning slightly traumatised fish into the river as easy prey for this expert underwater swimmer?

Mute Swans (no song, only hisses and snores of disapproval) probably pair for life and by the end of March will have re-established a river territory and driven out last year's brood. Eggs, however, are not usually laid until mid April. Ringing of Mute Swans (no connection with swan-upping) has been carried out from Oxford on considerable lengths of the middle Thames for many years. It is always worth looking for the large white plastic rings that have been used. Both legs carry a ring which has a letter and two numbers, plain to see, identifying each individual, which may then be observed carefully for evidence of fidelity to both a mate and a stretch of river over several years.

A special pleasure in March is to hear the first Chiffchaff of the year singing. Though a few Chiffchaffs overwinter in this country (and are seen at garden bird tables), the majority arrive this month and next from the south, many from as far away as northern Africa. Their song heralds the approaching arrival of all the other summer visitors and, however late the spring, assures one that winter is at last at an end.

The Titmice

Little Tommy Tittlemouse,
Lived in a little house;
He caught fishes
In other men's ditches.

Anon.

REAT, Blue, Coal, and Long-tailed Tits — or Titmice as they were once properly called — are those most often found in gardens, together with the Marsh Tit if the garden is on the edge of woodland. All are widespread in Britain, but there is also the Willow Tit, very like the Marsh and the least common; but both Marsh and Willow Tit are rather rare in gardens, and neither occurs in Ireland at all. The Long-tailed Tit usually prefers something wilder than a garden and is a quite different tit from the others — indeed some people think it may not be a tit at all, but more closely related to the babblers, most of which live nearer the equator than the British Isles.

The rarest British tit is the Crested Tit, which occurs only in open Scots pine forest and has become restricted to isolated patches in Scotland, notably in the relict Caledonian pine forest of the Cairngorms. This very limited distribution is surprising because the Crested Tit breeds in almost all suitable pine forests across Europe, and yet it does not spread into new plantations near its favourite sites in Scotland. It is a decorative bird with a pointed, speckled black-and-white crest.

The Blue Tit has a bright blue cap, but the others have black ones, though of different fashions, and the Coal Tit has a conspicuous white patch in the middle of its nape. All are in the genus *Parus*, which is its name in Latin, and together they form a group of engaging acrobats.

The Great Tit, aptly named as the largest of all our titmice, is also known as 'Ox Eye', a rather over-imaginative country name which presumes the profile of the bird's head resembles the large, placid eye of an Ox. It is also called 'Saw-sharpener' from the sawing-like call it gives, *teacher,teacher,teacher*. In fact the Great Tit has an extensive vocabulary of short calls and often imitates other birds, successfully deluding the listening bird-watcher.

The Blue Tit, on the other hand, has a more entertaining, sweetly soft song, *kiss-me-quick-cherry-erry-bee*. A common country name is 'Nun', because it supposedly seems to be wearing a hood, but it has a mouthful of other fanciful names. A blue tit it certainly is, a blue which is an even brighter aquamarine in the western North African countries. In the late 18th century, Gilbert White of Selborne called the Blue Tit "a great frequenter of houses and a general devourer". Delightfully, he goes on: "Besides insects, it is very fond of flesh; for it frequently picks bones on dung-hills : it is a vast admirer of suet, and haunts butchers' shops . . It will also . . be well entertained with the seeds on the head of a sunflower." How is it that such charming and evocative English is so rarely met with these days?

Great and Blue Tits are the vandals who pierce the milk bottle tops outside your kitchen door. The habit, first reported in the late 1940s, when the use of silvery tops became general, started in more than one place, apparently casually spreading out from each centre, and is now met with throughout the country. The development of such a habit is an example of 'insight learning', i.e. the tit, having had the temerity first to try to reach the cream, then has the insight to recognise all milk bottles as the source of this delicacy and that they can be found on doorsteps, most of which are safe to maraud in the early hours of daylight. In addition, the spread of the habit shows that imitation, the basis of learning, must play an important part in the daily life of birds, as in humans, else how could the practice have spread? Tits are seldom found singly and outside the breeding season travel round in small parties.

Catching and ringing them has shown that the 3-4 tits you may talk to at the winter bird table are not always the same individuals you thought they were. Not at all; well over 100 tits have been caught in one semi-rural garden in a single winter. The small parties of two, three, four or more birds which make regular visits together to the bird table are nomadic. They move round, probably on a regular trail which takes in many gardens, several dozen such parties going through the same areas during the winter, some of them recognisable for having had tiny aluminium or monel rings attached to their legs.

It is well known that tits take readily to nest-boxes, where they are usually very successful in rearing five or six young, or more. It is considerate to put boxes up in the garden, because natural holes in trees are not so common as all that. However, there is a hidden danger — young tits are quite often found dead in boxes put up in suburban gardens where there are not enough trees and shrubs from which to provide food, such as caterpillars, for the young. Another danger is to put up boxes that are wrongly designed. Squirrels and cats are just as good as tits at recognising them as nest sites, and if the entrance hole is not far enough above the nest material and its owner (not just the bottom of the box), a slim long arm from which there is no escape can stretch down and extract a helpless nestling or a brooding adult. The depth of a box should be nothing less than ten inches from the entrance hole to the floor. The direction in which the box should face is problematical, but it is best to avoid facing it towards the midday sun or the prevailing wind. However, an unaccepted nest box one year may be busily used another.

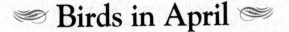

Birds in April

Whitethroat *Sylvia communis*

April, April,
Laugh thy girlish laughter;
Then, the moment after
Weep thy girlish tears

Sir W. Watson (1858-1935), *April*.

PRIL is a month of expectancy. There is an excitement in looking and listening for the first of our summer visitors returning from their far distant sunbaked homes. The Cuckoo, best known, and its first arrival often reported in letters in the national press together with that of the Swallow, both arrive about the middle of the month. The young Cuckoos left here last year after their parents had already gone abroad in August, and amazingly, with no prior knowledge, will have found their traditional favourite African winter quarters on their own. European Cuckoos winter all across tropical Africa, those from the British Isles mostly east of the big westerly bulge of Africa. There have been two British ringed birds recovered in Africa, one in Togo and one in Cameroun.

Perhaps most heartwarming in April is hearing the newly arrived warblers singing, their varied repertoires so different from our resident songsters, though the breeding season of nearly all of them will not be in full swing until the middle of next month. The Blackcap and Whitethroat in the genus *Sylvia*, those in the genus *Phylloscopus* like the Willow Warbler, Chiffchaff and Wood Warbler, and the Sedge and Reed Warblers in the *Acrocephalus* genus are fine examples. They will have wintered south of the Sahara, some 2,500 miles away. At one small marshy site by the Thames, bird-ringing has been in progress for over ten years and many individual Sedge and Reed Warblers ringed one year have been retrapped one, two, three and even four years later. Not only have they made these tremendous journeys, but they will have navigated, without any artificial aids, their return to exactly the same few square metres from which they migrated seven months earlier. Our Swallows will have travelled even further, for many of them move right down to South Africa for the winter. No wonder that our near ancestors seriously considered that they might hibernate, and, because they roosted in flocks in reedbeds overnight and had gone by next morning, they even considered that the birds plunged underwater into the mud to do so.

It is not known how these astounding journeys are successfully undertaken every year, but theories abound. A bird low in weight has been shown to add an extra 40% to its own body weight in a matter of 3-4 days, and it is essential for migrant birds that they store as much fat (fuel) as possible before they leave on long journeys. It has also been shown that the energy available from the fat thus stored by one of these tiny voyagers could, astonishingly, support it if necessary for a non-stop journey of over 36 hours! It is reserves of energy such as this which make it possible for them to cross the inhospitable deserts between the Equator and Europe and Asia where there are no places with tolerable conditions for the bird to land, if only for rest.

Besides these surprising physiological findings, there is the mystifying navigational ability of the long-distant migrant, which leaves its family acre to travel a return journey of 5,000 miles, quite unaided, before arriving back at its birth place seven months later. Very many of the small perching birds such as the warblers travel mainly by night, and there can be no doubt that the stars are their most important guides, proven for a few species in a planetarium. One theory holds that the bird's zenith, that is the point in the heavens vertically above its head, and its relation to the rotation of the heavenly sphere at any given time, is learned by sight at the birthplace while the bird is gaining its adult weight; but knowledge of the zenith of its winter quarters must be inherited. This winter zenith is a point in a pattern of stars recognisable any-where in the night sky at a particular time. There must in some cases be an intermediate zenith when the winter quarters are well below the equator, and therefore below the home horizon. For this theory to function the bird will need a reliable internal clock and the visual ability to recognise small changes of angle to the vertical, and it has indeed been shown that nocturnal migrants have anatomy and physiology for both these requirements. The main complication for such an hypothesis is, of course, the ever rotating night sky. That the problem is not insur-mountable, however, is evidenced by some nomadic desert tribes, who cross uncharted sandy wastes without any artificial aids, not even a compass, and reach their destination hundreds of miles away without difficulty. It has also been postulated that the "Three Kings of Orient" had a premonition that one particular star was to be at its zenith over the Messiah at his birth at a particular time and followed it until it was so — at Bethlehem. Who knows?

There is good proof that pigeons and waterfowl, at least, can recognise and correct flight directions from the angle of the sun, both in relation to the top of the sun's arc of movement across the sky and its angle above the horizon, and that they use such data for homing. Compass direction is probably only a rough help, merely giving a sense of general direction; navigation by compass cannot be successful on its own, since birds are easily driven off course by unruly weather and must then have an ability to recognise this and compensate for it.

Thirty years ago theories which involved magnetic lines on the earth's surface were consid-ered merely unlikely speculation; nevertheless it has now been shown conclusively that some birds can recognise changes in the magnetic fields through which they are passing, though how they do so, and how exactly they use this ability is as yet obscure. Even more surprisingly, smell, at least of conditions within easy reach of home, can play a part in helping pigeons to reach their cots. The truth inherent in all this research and speculation is that birds have several methods at their disposal for finding their way across vast distances.

It is humbling indeed to hold in one's hand a living creature weighing less than 15gm (about the weight of an ordinary letter) and to realise that this animated mite, happily nesting in the reed bed where it was born, or where it has previously nested, has travelled 2,500 miles, at least 600 of them over the bare sands of the Sahara Desert, perhaps to Timbuctoo or to Ghana and beyond, and the 2,500 miles back, possibly two, three, four or more times, all of 20,000 miles, in a lifetime, relying on no artificial aids and on its own tiny wings alone for transport. Whatever in future may be discovered, the achievements of these lively visitors will never be less than astonishing.

☙ The Cuckoo ☙

We loved
The sound of one another's voice more,
Than the grey cuckoo loves his name

Tennyson, *Lovers Tale.*

HE CUCKOO comes in April — usually in southern England about 13 April, at much the same time as other summer migrants. This has led to several birds, such as the Wryneck being given the name 'Cuckoo's Mate'. "In May he sings all day", sometimes unbrokenly as he patrols his territory, trying to attract a mate. The female has a bubbling call when excited, but never cries *cuckoo*. Once established as a pair, the female has a busy time searching with an expert eye for nests in which to lay her eggs, singly at a time. Each Cuckoo tends to specialise in the bird species which it parasitises, common sufferers being Dunnocks (Hedge Sparrows), Reed and Sedge Warblers, Pied Wagtails and Meadow Pipits. The search for and finding of the host's nest is intriguing. The female first spies from vantage points in the territory and when a possible host has been spotted visiting one particular place repeatedly, she goes searching there on foot, so to speak. Sadly, she is often unintentionally led to the nest itself by the victim's fiercely hostile behaviour when the enemy is at the gate, aggression becoming less when the Cuckoo is getting "colder" (as in the young child's game of "hunt the thimble"). Ironically, the 'bravery' of the small defendant only leads it to reveal what is being guarded so valiantly.

"In June he changes his tune", the hiccupping "cuk-cuk-cuckoo" now being heard more often than earlier in the year. This stuttering may coincide with the height of the breeding season, and can undoubtedly be due to over-excitement! By the end of June the female will have finished laying her quota of 8-12 eggs for the year. Cuckoos' eggs have provided the egg collector (before it became illegal to hold any collection of eggs without authority) with much interest and enjoyment, since they are so variable in colouring and patterning, depending much on the foster parent preferred by each individual bird. Those using the Dunnock, for example, have a bluish colouring; eggs from single individuals may be recognisable throughout their lives.

The eggs are small for a bird of the Cuckoo's size, suitably matching the unfortunate host's. Only one is normally deposited in each foster home, since the successful upbringing of more than one huge, ravenous nestling 2-3 times the nest owner's size and weight is unlikely. There used to be great controversy about how the Cuckoo deposited its egg in the foster parent's nest, causing much ill-will and abuse at ornithological gatherings of the time. The Rev. F.C.R. Jourdain, an eminent ornithologist and elite oologist (egg collector), acquired the reputation of a belligerent and outspoken adversary in any ornithological discussion, and in particular during disputes about how a Cuckoo placed its egg in any particular nest. So aggressive, in fact, did he become on several occasions that he deservedly acquired the (scientific) nickname *Pastor pugnax*. The controversy was finally resolved only when cine-photography was able to show the Cuckoo in the act of laying its egg direct into the nest of the host, the method now recognised as being usual. The female does usually pick up one of the host's eggs before laying her own — which generally takes only about ten seconds — and may be seen carrying it away, giving rise to the now discarded theory that the egg was laid on the ground and carried to the host's nest.

Survival required that the nestling Cuckoo hatch out first, and so a short incubation period for the egg has evolved. The nestling, hideous, blind and naked, within a few hours of hatching is restlessly pushing around amongst the eggs at the bottom of the nest until a rival's egg lodges in a specially evolved and sensitive hollow in its back. Then, aided by outspread featherless wings and braced legs, it manoeuvres backwards up the side of the nest, finally tipping the irritating object out over the edge to oblivion. An exhausting process. It continues with its restless 'ethnic cleansing' until all the eggs are disposed of and it is free to rest and monopolise its foster parents' attentions. What a start to life! Speaking anthropomorphically, it must be agreed that this demanding and ruthless child has achieved its survival, albeit unknowingly, by its own great exertions at only a few hours old. Its exertions will continue, mainly as gestures unmistakeably emphasising the need to satisfy an enormous appetite. By the time it fledges it will have exhausted its foster parents almost beyond endurance, but there are few records to show how the unlucky hosts fare in the future.

The young Cuckoo can, however, like other species' young, be admired, even commended, for its ability when fully grown to leave home unaccompanied (its real parents having already gone abroad) on an unrehearsed journey, and to navigate well over 3,000 miles to its winter quarters in Africa, arriving at the right place at the right time, next year to return to the same fields where it was born. It is indeed more than commendable, it is astonishing.

The Wryneck

ἰυγξ ἕλκε τὺ τῆνον ἐμὸν ποτὶ δῶμα τὸν ἄνδρα.

(*Jynx, hither wind home to me my lover*)

Theocritus, *Simætha*.

ADLY, the Wryneck *Jynx torquilla* no longer breeds anywhere in the British Isles, except that very occasionally a pair is found nesting in central Scotland, a relict population, originating possibly in Scandinavia. The cause of this decline is unaccounted for, but numbers are fewer all over Europe, which suggests that some major factor is at work, such as small, but evidently significant, changes in the average temperatures across the northern part of the northern hemisphere. Such changes occur very slowly, measured in tenths of a degree, and several such fluctuations have been scientifically recorded over recent centuries — they have nothing in common with the present so-called greenhouse effect. It is probable that the life cycle and food chain of the Wryneck's staple diet, ants' eggs and larvae, are affected.

This decline was well indicated by the bird's status in Goring-on-Thames. Forty years ago a pair bred probably annually in the garden of a large house there — they are very tenacious of nest sites, returning year after year to exactly the same nest hole. In 1948, at another site, a male came and 'sang' for three weeks and then was heard no more except on one day the next year. This was the Wryneck's last appearance in Goring, and exemplified the disappearance of this once quite common bird; during the next 30 years it totally ceased to breed anywhere in England. Its summer appearances in all counties became fewer and fewer as it retreated further and further into the southeast corner of Kent, where were the great areas of fruit farming which had been its main breeding stronghold. On the Continent it has always been a commoner bird and its decline has been less readily noticeable, though nonetheless probably just as severe.

It is a handsome bird, the Wryneck, well camouflaged and elusive, though with a loud 'song', a rapidly repeated rather querulous *quee-quee-quee-.....quee*, the first three calls on a rising scale, followed by as many as ten or a dozen similar notes in succession. The call is far carrying, seeming especially so at dawn to a bird-watcher trespassing in a stranger's garden. It is very like that of some falcons, and even eminent ornithologists at a congress in Finland some years ago were repeatedly deceived by the cries of a Hobby, which they took to be those of a Wryneck. Calling stops when the egg-laying is complete. The clutch may be sometimes as many as ten eggs. Many years ago, one female, puir lass (it was in Scotland), had her daily laid egg removed by an experimenter and only gave up when she had laid the huge total of over 40.

Slim, rather smaller than a Thrush, bigger than a Robin, the plumage is mottled and streaked, vermiculated in browns and buff, greys and black, showing a smart checkerboard pattern on the main flight feathers at rest. The grey back has a dark diamond-shaped patch across the centre of the shoulders, extending onto the nape, somehow recalling the markings on the shoulders of a donkey. Altogether an attractive though inconspicuous attire.

The Wryneck is a member of the woodpecker family, though a very distinctive and atypical one. It has the two toes facing forwards and two back, which is the main distinguishing feature of the family, and it climbs tree trunks like a woodpecker, but is equally at ease perched across a branch. Like the Green Woodpecker, it is a ground feeder, picking up ants' eggs and larvae by exceedingly rapid extrusions of its long, thin, coiled tongue. It nests in holes in trees, so that old fruit orchards were always a favourite habitat. Certainly the Wryneck would not be at home today in the small thin-trunked orchards without any ants in a modern fruit farm — but the new farming methods came after the drop in its numbers had already started.

Jynx figures largely in Greek mythology, and *torquilla* is a diminutive of the Latin *torquere*, to twist. The name *torquilla* is deservedly applied to the Wryneck. As its English name emphasises, this unusual bird has the habit, particularly when disturbed on its nest, or indeed in any stress situation, of explosively letting out a fierce hissing noise while it writhes its neck in distorting, twisting movements — a performance that is intended to frighten away predators, and could easily be taken for the dangerous fury of a snake.

The Wryneck having once been so common, has many country names related to its habits and migrations. 'Writhe-neck' and 'Snake bird' derive from its contortions and hissing when disturbed. 'Cuckoo's mate' is no more than a reference to its arrival in the same week as the Cuckoo, but in Hampshire the 'Cuckoo whit' was said, somewhat mysteriously, to order his coat at Beaulieu Fair (15 April) and put it on at Downton Fair (23 April). Certainly its arrival date in nearby Oxfordshire used always to be close to 15 April. 'Barley bird' relates to its arrival when spring barley was being sown. In about 1930, an old man at Frensham on the Hants/Surrey border, was still referring to the Wryneck as 'Barking bird', because it returned home when the felled oaks needed to have their bark stripped.

> "In an upper room of her mother's house in St Omar sat the fair
> Torfrida, alternately looking out of the window and at a book of mechanics.
> In the garden outside, the wryneck (as his fashion in May) was calling
> Pi-pi-pi among the gooseberry bushes, till the cobwalls rang again. In the
> book was a Latin recipe for drying the poor wryneck, and using him as a
> filtre which should compel the love of any person desired."

So wrote Charles Kingsley in *Hereward the Wake* in 1865, setting the scene in relation to this bird's place in mythology, one that is fascinating and open to contradictory interpretations.

In c.490 B.C. Pindar tells how the Argonauts fought the Kolchians, thereafter settling down to their usual violent lovers' intrigues, during which Aphrodite appears and, for reasons unknown, introduces the idea of binding "Jynx" to a 4-spoked wheel, to be used like a prayer wheel. She was trying to help Jason to obtain the love of Medea, who at the time was resisting his attentions, thus honouring her promises to her parents — an unusual state of affairs obviously calling for the use of unusual magic. Why Pindar chose to specify "Jynx" for this unpleasant ritual is pure speculation, but the bird was presumably common and its tortuous writhings evidently known and worthy of having mystical powers. "Jynx" was only identified as the Wryneck much later by Aristotle in c.280 B.C., so that in 1766, Linnaeus, who always dug into the classics for the scientific name of any creature, found *Jynx* an obvious choice for the Wryneck.

In the third century B.C. "the wits of Alexandria" recorded many myths about Jynx. One of these made out that Jynx was the daughter of a goddess, who for the benefit of her friend Io, a priestess of Hera at Argos, put a love spell on Zeus. This misplaced devotion was quickly spotted by Hera, Zeus's wife, who in fury turned the innocent Jynx into the Wryneck. In another sorry tale, the King of Pieria had nine daughters who were the apples of his eye, so much so that the poor deluded parent rashly challenged the nine muses to a song and dance contest on Mount Helikon. Inevitably the Muses won, and for their presumption Pierus's nine sweet maidens were turned into birds, of which the Wryneck was one. Did unhappy Pierus thereafter put up a large bird table in his garden?

Theocritus tells a tale, in which a poor young girl, Simaetha, pines for her estranged loved one, Delphis, a macho athlete. Desperately and without parental permission, she braves the night with her maidservant, terrified both of promised magic and of discovery. The rites are elegantly described, including heartfelt pleadings to Jynx to "draw back her lover". Sadly, this courage and belief were unrewarded.

In this poem "Jynx" has been translated as "Bird-wheel" and in illustrations, Eros, the god of love, often carried a 4-spoked wheel, a predecessor of that popular toy of schoolboys, the whirligig. Strung on a circle of string through the two central holes of the hub of the wheel, the string can be twisted and then by pulling to and fro made to revolve rapidly first in one direction, then in the reverse. The wheel's mystique, with or without the Wryneck, has led to two main, but quite opposed, conclusions. In the 1880s, one Bury, a classicist, by very involved reasoning derived Jynx from Io, the Moon Goddess, asserting that *io* is similar to the Wryneck's call, which it undoubtedly is not. Nevertheless the Jynx wheel was used sometimes in lunar rights — indeed poor Simaetha deliberately chose a night with a full moon for her desperate appeal. Some 30 years later, Dr Cook refuted all Dr Bury's ideas and associated the jynx wheel with the sun, the sun being long represented by a 4-spoked wheel. Cook further showed that solar wheels were often adorned with the wings of birds and one or more snakes. The Wryneck therefore appeared to him to be "a most desirable appendage".

There are no marks for guessing which supposition is most likely. It is even possible that Theocritus merely found that "Jynx" fitted more readily into his ode than any other object, but it is surely undeniable that the pursuit of birds leads one down many enjoyable sidetracks which it would have been a pity to have missed.

Wryneck *Jynx torquilla*, from *Illustrated Manual of British Birds*, 1889.

Birds in May

Chaffinch *Fringilla coelebs*

"O blackbird, what a boy you are!
How you do go it
Blowing your bugle to that one sweet star—
How you do blow it!

And does she hear you, blackbird boy, so far?
Or is it wasted breath?
"Good Lord! she is so bright
To-night!"
The blackbird saith."

T.E. Brown, *Vespers*.

AY DAY morning and the choir of Magdalen College, Oxford, mounts its famous tower to join the dawn chorus of birds. A boys' voice choir puts one in mind of the joyous, innocent sounds of a multitude of birds singing as the sun rises above the horizon. Though not about the dawn chorus, Edward Thomas wrote:

"And for that moment a Blackbird sang
Close by, and round him, mistier,
Farther and farther, all the birds
Of Oxfordshire and Gloucestershire."

To find oneself at 5.30am on a warm May morning, when the sky is changing from a dusky grey to a golden light, seated on a grassy slope near a wood, away from man-made sounds, listening to a serenade from a hundred tiny throats — is an exhilarating moment. Quite unforgettable. One seems to sense that the singers are wrapped up in their performance, nothing but personal danger can stop it, it is compulsive — and rather beautiful.

·Some birds, like the Chaffinch, will have learned their song during their first ever summer. At first one hears a poor version of its *chip-chip-cherry-erry-erry- tissi-tchew-ee-o*, sometimes likened to a spin-bowler's prancing run up to the wicket to bowl. There is a Chaffinch dialect in France (where they never play cricket) of the same song in which there is an extra exclamation at the end, as it might be "howzat?". Most small birds appear not to need any practice. Of our three summer visiting 'leaf warblers', the Willow Warbler has a wistful tinkling of descending notes ending in a whisper, in contrast to its close relative the Chiffchaff with its repeated chant *chiff-chaff, chiff-chaff, chif-chi-chiff-chaff, chiff-chaff*....... for up to a minute or more on end. The less common Wood Warbler's trilling has been compared to the sound of an old silver threepenny bit spinning on its edge and toppling over to a standstill on a marble slab. All these self-absorbed soloists of the dawn chorus are advertising their territories and strengthening a pair bond — before breakfast. But the anthropomorphic will say that they indeed do it with enjoyment, and who is to deny them?

Recognising that song has the function of advertising, whether for possession of a territory or of a mate, and that its intention is to maintain the male's hold on both (for the bird's world can be a very competitive one), makes it more realistic to describe other sounds used for the same purpose as song. There is no music about the mechanical drumming of a woodpecker, even when it chooses to drum on a hollow metal object, but its reverberations have the same intentions as the song of a warbler. Another mechanically produced 'song' and a rather pleasing one is the bleating sound given by a Snipe for the same purpose. It was not until about 70 years ago that it was shown how the Snipe created the noise. In the spring, the male will fly rapidly round in great circles at quite a height, covering a large area in which somewhere well hidden is its mate or nest. It had been long noticed that the sound was only produced when the bird suddenly plunged very steeply on a quite short but rapid slant. Eventually it was discovered that the bleat could be produced by fixing the two outer tail feathers of the Snipe to a cork, spread wide apart. and the cork then whirled round rapidly on the end of string. The first demonstration came at the end of a convivial ornithological dinner in a London hotel and brought the house down.

The Woodpigeon's song is of yet another type, of rather friendly, fulsome, rounded cooing notes, common to all the doves. Interestingly, and not usually recognised, the intervals between the notes of its well-known phrase are misleading. *Take two cows David, take two* is the best known interpretation of its song, but careful listening shows that this advice in fact ends with the second *take* and begins with *Two*. There is a misleading pause after *David* which is longer than the next pause after *take* and than those which separate the other notes from each other, as if a new repetition of the phrase was beginning — i.e. the pause between complete phrases is shorter than that between notes. The song's interpretation should read *Two . cows . David . . . take /. Two . cows . David . . . take /*. It is no more easy to hear than to describe.

Some years ago, a musician, Joan Hall-Craggs, with very acute hearing, expertly trained, and knowledgeable about birds, patiently recorded one particular Blackbird, amongst others, every morning for up to two hours from dawn for many weeks on end during the nesting season, and again over the next two years. Her patience and painstaking analysis were well rewarded. Of great significance in more than the purely ornithological field was her revelation that the usual short phrases created by this bird (as well as by other Blackbirds) were arranged, re-arranged, discarded or replaced by new ones over the weeks until a most-favoured sequence or repertoire was gradually composed. Her skill was also such that she was able to recognise by ear several Blackbirds individually by their choice of phrases, even from one year to the next — a remarkable discovery and achievement.

The Kingfisher

As kingfishers catch fire, dragonflies draw flame

Gerard Manley Hopkins, *Spring and Fall.*

HE DAZZLING KINGFISHER *Alcedo atthis* is all too rarely glimpsed, often only as a flash of iridescent azure-blue speeding down the river, piping as it goes, more frequently, I like to think, when it is approaching a bend. At rest it is even harder to see, perched on a branch protruding over the water's edge, though one may then discern the chestnut-red underparts and the bright, speckled black and blue crown. With luck one may catch it as it plunges deep into the water, to emerge with a fish, which it will then thrash repeatedly against its perch to subdue it into a state fit to be swallowed easily, head first.

Like others of our resident birds, Kingfishers have suffered badly in the last few decades from changes in stream and river management and from water pollution. They are, unfortunately, also very susceptible to severe winters, such as that in 1962/3, which took a heavy toll of their numbers. On the other hand, quick recovery occurs where its preferred habitats are undisturbed and food is plentiful, since as many as three successful broods are sometimes raised in one year. Throughout the British Isles there are at present about 10,000 pairs, which may suggest plenty. But the total is in fact a very modest one for the area involved — there are many tens of thousands of miles of suitable streams and brooks, as well as rivers and gravel pits, where Kingfishers could feed and find banks in which to tunnel their nests.

It is mistaken to think that all kingfishers live up to the name. There are over 80 different species worldwide, many of which never see a fish. Some eat only spiders and other arachnids; others enjoy lizards as their main food, and yet others a diet of mixed insects only. Many live in rain forests and woodlands far from running or standing water. Like our own Kingfisher they are all conspicuously coloured, blue usually predominating, though there is a group which is purely black and white. Size differences in the family are considerable. The African Dwarf Kingfisher weighs a mere 8gm, half that of the Robin; while the heaviest weighs in at over 500gm, the Laughing Kookaburra of Australia, somehow a surprise member of the kingfisher family and one which does not rely on fish at all. All nest in holes, our Kingfisher excavating its own long tunnel into sandy or earth banks, in some cases up to a metre long. The forest dwellers and the large species nest in holes in trees, and even termite mounds are not uncommonly used.

The kingfisher family has been divided into several genera, which of course required to be given scientific names. In the past, as now, these names were in Latin or the Latinised form of a Greek word. But authors, keen to display their knowledge of classical literature, often used a mythological source for inspiration. *Halcyon* was one of the earliest names, embracing many members of the family. Halcyon, or Alcyone, was a daughter of Aeolus, the guardian of the winds, and married Ceyx, son of Lucifer, the Morning-star. Regrettably this love-match gave Alcyone, so deep was her love, the temerity recklessly to compare the pair of them to Hera and the great god Zeus. Inevitably Zeus found this irksome and flung a thunderbolt at a ship on which Ceyx was sailing to consult the oracle at Claros, and drowned him. Alcyone who had been told in a dream of her husband's fate was devastated and threw herself into the sea to join her lover. Out of pity, the gods transformed both of them into kingfishers. Hence, two scientific names in the kingfisher family are *Halcyon* and *Ceyx*. *Alcedo*, another generic name, is rather more prosaic, being derived direct from the Latin for a kingfisher, and one humorist used its anagram *Dacelo* for a close relation! On the other hand, Atthis, a pretty young woman from the island of Lesbos and a favourite of Sappho, took the fancy of another author, who used *atthis* as a specific name for our Kingfisher. O! classical days.

A celebrated myth related by Virgil in the *Georgics* says that the Kingfisher once, having made her nest out of fishbones, launched it on the sea, there to lay and incubate her eggs and bring up the young in the fabled halcyon days, during which time it was ordained by a divine command that "the whole ocean should be stayed". One is somehow reminded of that kind policeman who annually had to halt traffic round London's Parliament Square while a Mallard and her string of downy ducklings passed safely to or from St James's Park. One can accept less readily a belief in Brittany that the dazzling Kingfisher is much given to swearing. Shame !

∾ The Swallow ∾

"..... that wondrous stone which the swallow
Brings from the shore of the sea to restore the sight of its fledglings; ....."

Longfellow, *Evangelise*.

E MAY THINK of the Swallow *Hirundo rustica* as the only swallow there is, and indeed it is referred to in almost all European literature and old handbooks as "the" Swallow. However that may be, there are in fact 73 other species of swallows and martins world wide, amongst them the attractively named Violet-Green, Golden, Welcome, Wire-tailed, Blue, and Mosque Swallows. The family is that of the Hirundinidae (-idae is the suffix indicating a family), and it is the subfamily Hirundininae (-inae for all subfamilies) that embraces the swallows and martins. There is, no great scientific difference between swallows and martins as a whole, though hirundines with a squarish, slightly concave end to the tail are more often referred to as martins, like our House Martin, while those with a more deeply forked tail like our own Swallow, with its elegant streamers, are termed swallows. In vernacular or national names the two words have sometimes been reversed — the Sand Martin of Britain, for instance, is called the Bank Swallow in the USA. But what's in a name?

Our Swallow and House Martin are amongst the most attractive and graceful of our summer visitors and, with the Cuckoo, are certainly given the most welcome. Indeed they are sadly missed when they fail to appear one spring in the shed or garage, or under the eaves of the house where they may have nested for many decades. As for so many of our summer migrants, fewer and fewer of them come home each year, and where there may have been perhaps three pairs of Swallows sharing the nesting amenities of a large barn, or 5-6 or more House Martins crowding into a favourite stretch of eaves, there may now be none at all. Under the broad eaves of one particular house in Portugal in the 1960s there were over 50 House Martins's nests crowded together, three deep; and a few years ago over 500 nests were counted in an almost continuous line round the airport building at Thessolonika in Greece. Nearer home, 430 to over 500 nests were counted under the five arches of the old bridge at Clifton Hampden in Berkshire in the 1950s. There are unlikely to be anything like these numbers now in any one of these places — indeed there are none or only one or two at Clifton Hampden today.

An inkling of the difficulties encountered by these long-distance migrants was given by the sad discovery once of a flock of some hundred Swallows, all dead, in an abandoned shed in the northern Algerian desert. Here they must have taken shelter from unrelenting heat or perhaps a dust storm, only to die there of thirst or hunger or exhaustion, after covering a great distance of hard-slogging travel, still miles and miles from the end of one of their hazardous twice yearly crossings of the Sahara Desert. Perhaps some of them were from your own homestead.

For such a common and well recognised bird, there are naturally many legends and unlikely beliefs. In the medical field, its ashes were used for such as "falling sickness", "blear eyes", in the latter case being mixed with honey and used externally, while blood from under the left wing also had remedial value for eye trouble. Veneration for the Swallow was widespread and it was considered unlucky to kill one, indeed doing so would turn cow's milk to blood. Yet in Ireland it was called "devil's bird" in some places, as it was believed that everyone had a hair on their head which, if plucked off by a Swallow, would condemn the victim to suffer eternal perdition. Oh dear, Oh dear!

More pleasantly, the Swallows' main arrival is about the middle of April. They stay on till September and early October. If they have been lucky with the weather each pair will have brought up two broods of 4-5 young. They are aerial feeders, gliding and swooping through the air catching insects; but in a cold wet summer insect life is much reduced — what is ideal for Swallows, as well as ourselves, is hot dry weather, with what rain is needed for a good growth of grass and vegetation, in which insects may thrive, coming only at night. On hot days, when the warm air has carried the insects up several hundred feet, there will the swallows and martins and swifts be also. On wet days the insects fly closely above the vegetation and Swallows will be seen skimming low over the ground in their pursuit. This, of course, has given rise to a country belief that if Swallows fly low the weather will be cold and wet; but, as often with country lore forecasts, cause and effect have been reversed.

The Swallow's return to its individual home of last year is always a happy talking point. What deserves more realisation is that this vulnerable elfin creature has just flown a massive 6,000 miles and more, probably from the southern half of southern Africa, flying by day (and by night if no tolerable conditions for roosting are in reach) on a broad, spread out front, over industrial complexes and cities, tropical forest, savanna, the widest parts of the barren Sahara sands, mountains and sea, with no navigation aids except its own built-in abilities. This phenomenal capacity to find the way so regularly and so accurately over such vast distances is still an unresolved mystery, and for man a truly humbling realisation of the superb abilities of these tiny members of the natural world. When they are ready to set off to their winter home, they will gather together in flocks. When you see a crowd of them on a roof top or spread out preening, resting in rows on telephone wires, or feeding to and fro over a pond, wish them good luck — they deserve it and may well need it.

Birds in June

Lapwing *Vanellus vanellus*

> A noise like of a hidden brook
> In the leafy month of June
> That to the sleeping woods all night
> Singeth a quiet tune
>
> Samuel Taylor Coleridge, *The Ancient Mariner.*

UNE is a hectic time for parent birds trying to bring their broods up to independence, and even more exhausting for those that immediately renew courtship and nest building for a second brood. It is sad to think that much of this endeavour ends, by next spring, in only one or two survivors from perhaps as many as eight eggs, sufficient merely to maintain the population at its present level. Natural wastage from cold, disease, accident and predators is a dismal reality.

Game bird young, such as Pheasant, Partridge and Snipe, as well as Lapwing and other plovers and shorebirds, are nidifugous and precocial — in plain English they leave the nest very shortly after hatching and are capable of walking and running and feeding themselves almost at once, like Sam 'n Ella, our farmyard chicks. So one needs a bit of luck to find one-day-old chicks. A Snipe's well hidden nest may be stumbled on by chance in the top of a grassy tussock in a damp meadow, betrayed by the parent panicking off when one is only a metre away, zig-zagging at speed, scolding *scape scape*; and there in a grassy cup are four chocolate-chestnut, downy, black-lined little bodies, tapestry patterned, motionless and totally vulnerable. Quite involuntarily one takes an indrawn breath of astonished pleasure.

The young of perching birds, including all our garden birds, are nidicolous and altricial — confined to the nest after hatching and in a helpless state, blind for several days, quite hideously naked, with sparse puny bits of down sticking up here and there and huge gaping mouths. Seen at a day old, it seems unbelievable that they can survive to become independent in some four weeks time.

In wet cold summers, when insects and caterpillars are at a premium, survivors may be very few. This is particularly so, as gamekeepers know only too well, for the downy free running chicks of game birds, which depend on warm sunny weather in June to reach a more hardy age. Their plight and that of partridges in particular is in no way helped by the widespread destruction of hedges in the last few decades. It is cheering, however, to read that there is some movement today for the re-creation and layering of hedges, as well as for the maintenance of old, often centuries old, hedgerows. All of this can do nothing but good for local bird populations, and if there is some inconvenience to harvesters there is also as much obligation for the preservation of ancient hedges as there is for the preservation of ancient buildings.

In June one is more likely to see more bathing by birds, mostly in the interests of hygiene but also to help in keeping cool. Nearly all birds water bathe, but some, like our House Sparrow, prefer to dust bathe. Total immersion is generally avoided, but it is common to see Blackbirds giving themselves a really good soaking. When wallowing, water flies everywhere. Standing in the bath, the head is held up and the spread tail totally submerged, while water is scattered by flapping vigorously one wing at a time while the body feathers are thoroughly ruffled. It is quite a party. Choosing the best time for such activity is important because conditions need to be right for the drying and preening that must follow before the bird's wet bedraggled feathers are again in proper order for its safety. Mere damping of the plumage is often preferred and then the bird will stand on the edge of the water, thrust its head down and splash the water over its back, shaking its wings and body the while. Sometimes one sees the bird jumping in and out of the water very quickly if the water is shallow enough. Swifts and Swallows will deliberately get themselves wet by flying just enough into the surface of the water to make a spray, while Kingfishers may plunge once, twice or more times into deep water. Some of the lark and parrot families living in dry countries will bathe in rain when opportunity offers, and some species dampen themselves by rubbing their feathers on wet or dew-covered foliage. The dampness or soaking makes the oiling and preening that follow easier and rids the bird of powdery dry skin flakes and even of parasites. Almost all birds have an oil gland, situated above the base of the tail, but its size and importance are not always as one would expect — it is large, of course, in water birds, but it is also large in the Wren, yet small in the Woodpigeon despite, or perhaps because of, its exceptionally thick coat of body feathers.

These habits are important because a bird becomes more vulnerable to many dangers if it is not in first class condition. Much pleasure can be found in providing the wherewithal in which birds can bathe in your garden. It takes all sorts to have a bath.

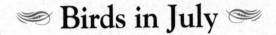

Blackbird *Turdus merula*

The English winter — ending in July,
To recommence in August.

George Gordon, Lord Byron   *Don Juan.*

T THE END of a stressful summer fraught with agonising over the children's exam results, overwork and revision, struggles with their proper feeding, disturbed nights, examination depression, celebrations, drowning of sorrows, what parent would not feel a fair sense of relief as he or she says goodbye to the last of the brood leaving on an extended holiday abroad, away from it all in luxurious sunshine?

It is much the same in July for most of our garden and other perching birds. For three months or so parent birds have been engaged in search for a happy environment for their young not yet born, in defending such territory, in courting and rivalry, home hunting, especially the hole nesters, followed by furnishing and egg laying and its essential preliminaries, the feeding and house-keeping needed during brooding — and then the unrelenting business of hygiene and keeping the growing youngsters clean well nourished, disciplined and safe. To go through all this twice, and in some species like the House Sparrow and Blackbird three times, in one summer is understandably exhausting. Parent birds will have lost weight and be carrying many damaged feathers by early August, the result of entanglements with foliage, sustained maybe in headlong escape from a predator such as the hedge-hopping Sparrowhawk. All this endeavour, struggle and mayhem must fairly suddenly become a thing of the past when the young have dispersed, and though the birds will not recognise it as their human counterparts might, the comparative peace and quiet allows time and opportunity for batteries to be recharged.

Breeding seasons are geared to making the most of preferred food supplies when these are at their most plentiful. Failure of a caterpillar population, for example, can bring fatal distress to many birds. An unusual example of this timing is provided by Eleonora's Falcon, a Mediterranean hawk named after the 14th century heroine of Sardinia's struggle for independence from Aragon, who, forwardly looking, laid down laws protecting birds of prey, partly it must be said for the benefit of falconry, her favourite sport. Like other falcons, Eleonora's feeds almost entirely on small birds such as our summer migrants. These migrate in autumn across the Mediterranean on their way south and are then a readily available source of food. Consequently Eleonora's Falcons postpone their breeding season from summer to early autumn to take advantage of this abundance, and the remains of many small song birds have been found and identified in their cliff nests in August and September. Some of the little corpses have carried rings on their legs, providing valuable information about their travels — it is pleasing to think that they have not died anonymously but have added a smidgen to our knowledge about their migration.

After the last young have dispersed from home, the remaining adults take their ease and have a well-earned rest, in much the same way as holiday makers on the beaches of the Costa del Sol or Acapulco, but in a much less ostentatious way; indeed positively secretively, since their autumn moult deprives them of the agility needed when in danger and they therefore skulk and hide. What a contrast!

July can be a month when few birds are to be seen. However, when the young have become confident and the adults have regained their weight and grown essential new feathers, they start moving across country in the direction of their winter homes in the south. Much increased activity is to be seen at the end of July and in August, especially at sites on the coast where visitors from the north make landfall after crossing the North Sea, or whither disorientated or storm driven birds may find safety, including rarities from as far distant as Siberia. It can be an exciting time for birdwatchers.

The Swift

To mark the Swift in rapid giddy ring
Dash round the steeple, unsubdued of wing

Gilbert White, *The Naturalist's Summer Evening Walk.*

HE SWIFT has beautifully evolved. It has a slim streamlined body, a stubby head with a mouth that has a huge gape for feeding while in flight, and a short and slightly forked tail. The narrow wings are swept back, scythe-shaped, ideal for slicing through the air in pursuit of its aerial prey, and at times they move so rapidly that the wings appear to beat alternately. The entire plumage is sooty black, except for a whitish throat.

The Swift is a prime example of adaptation to an almost entirely air-borne existence. It collects all its food in flight, from which it also obtains all the fluid it needs. Indeed, it is always wheeling through the air except when it lands at its nest site or alights to roost. There is evidence that mating and even sleeping occurs while in the heavens. Mating takes place mostly on the nest, but it has also been reliably observed on the wing. The Reverend Gilbert White of Selborne writing in September 1774 about this possibility writes about a flock of Swifts high overhead: ". . every now and then one [may] drop on the back of another, and both of them sink down together for many fathoms with a loud piercing shriek. This I take to be the juncture when the business of generation is carrying on." How wonderfully expressed!

As to its roosting on the wing, the evidence is mostly circumstantial. Flocks of birds have been seen on fine evenings rising at dusk from the aerial space around a nesting colony, such as a church tower, and ascending almost out of sight. These ascents are presumably of breeding adults and unmated birds; but the breeders are seen to peel off and return to their nests as the light dims, while the others fly higher and higher until no longer visible in the fading light; nor do they return — in fact there are no records of birds entering a nest after dark. In addition, the screaming cries of Swifts have often been heard at night, coming from considerable heights, and birds have been seen returning from on high to the neighbourhood of a colony at dawn.

Further evidence has come from radar. Birds in flocks can be picked up by suitable radar and appear as moving shadows ('angels') on the screen. By combining what can be seen by the eye with the radar, sudden appearances of 'angels' have been observed at dawn at considerable altitude, well away from the neighbourhood of any likely earthbound roost. Breeding pairs roost routinely at the nest. On migration, the birds roost communally, clinging upright to vertical surfaces such as walls or cliffs, or occasionally the outer foliage of a tree. In especially cold weather at any time of year, very many may cluster together, closely packed, undoubtedly in order to preserve body heat, a habit well known in bees, and not unknown in humans.

The American Chimney Swift, a relative of our Common Swift, both nests and roosts in chimneys and hollow trees, in vast numbers. Audubon, the celebrated painter of American birds, over 150 years ago examined a 60ft hollow tree and estimated it contained 9,000 Chimney Swifts. The base of the tree-trunk was over 5ft wide and he relates how he cut a hole into it, crawled through the deep and smelly litter of droppings, and with a torch saw the birds clinging side by side to the interior. Returning before dawn, he listened with his ear against the trunk. After waiting about 20 minutes he heard a terrific rushing sound which made him jump back-wards, thinking the tree must be crashing down; but it was merely the swifts leaving the roost *en masse* from a hole at the top of the tree to start their day. The Swift's name is not a misnomer; it can probably attain a speed of 40mph in level flight and of course greater speeds in a prolonged dive. Such a speed is exciting enough as it stands, but in relation to the body-size of a Swift this rate is prodigious. To keep it in perspective, consider the tiny body of a fly — to state that it is travelling at 40mph is quite unmeaningful. The difficulty in comparing the rates of these two very dissimilar bodies is that there appears to be no measure of speed related to the size of the moving body. There is a need to create a new concept of speed, let us say a 'monk', comparable to a knot, well known as the rate of an object when passing through a distance of one nautical mile in one hour. One monk could be defined as the rate at which an object passes through one length of its own body in one second. Thus an object passing through a distance of say three times the length of its body in one second is travelling at three monks. A vehicle travelling at 60mph covers 88ft per second; supposing it to be 8ft long it is then doing 11 monks. A fly, however, one tenth of an inch long covering 10 inches in one second is going at the rate of 100 monks; at 60mph it would be doing 10,560 monks. This goes some way to making a more comprehensible comparison of the relative speeds of objects of vastly different size. The comparison is meaningful. The Swift flying at 40mph covers nearly 60ft per second. The length of a Swift's body (for simplicity excluding the tail) is half one foot. So its body, travelling at 60ft per second, is doing 120 monks — that is, it travels a distance of 120 times its own length in one second. Top sprinters at their fastest are moving at about 20mph, say 30ft per second, that is (given their body 'length' in the vertical position is one foot from front to back) only 30 monks. The Swift's speed is therefore indeed prodigious, and its ability at perhaps only a quarter of that speed, say 30 monks, to steer accurately into a narrow slit under the eaves of a house onto its nest ledge, is indeed awe-inspiring. It requires both split second timing and very rapid changes of focus (well beyond the human eye's ability) as it rushes towards the site entrance. In addition there is the sudden braking necessary, accompanied by wing closure, to secure a safe landing on its short legs on the chosen ledge. We should never cease to be amazed.

A charming characteristic of our Swift is its indulgence in screaming parties, which occur at any time through the season, especially on warm summer evenings. Parties will join together and tear around screaming to each other, weaving wonderfully intricate flight patterns, avoiding collisions with no evident difficulty, even in the close quarters of a college quadrangle. It is forgivable to think that it is a friendly social get together for sheer enjoyment — a screaming party passing a nesting colony will tempt out the nesting pairs, and all join in a riotous tearabout. What fun! A lovely bird.

The Mute Swan

Man comes, and tills the fields, and lies beneath,
And after many a summer dies the Swan.

Alfred, Lord Tennyson, *Tithonus*.

 HE MUTE SWAN *Cygnus olor*, an imperial bird. It is easily recognised by its grand size and the purity of its wholly white plumage; by its elegant long arched neck and a commanding head, a bright orange bill with a prominent black knob at its base, from which extends a black line to the eye and down the back edge of the bill — it is this feature which produces its severely stern, haughty look. The cob, as the male is called, has a rather more prominent knob than the female or pen, and has the duty, performed very firmly, of protecting his territory against trespassers to ensure the safety of his mate and of their young, the cygnets sometimes as many as ten of them. When the mental trauma of matrimony and parenthood are absent, quite large congregations of Swans occur, such as the flocks at Caversham Bridge, Reading. Exceptionally too, Swans will breed in colonies, usually when semi-domesticated; perhaps the most famous is the swannery at Abbotsbury, at the west end of the Chesil Beach in Dorset, where the numbers have sometimes been in the hundreds. There, however, they were originally used as a food supply for the Benedictine monks of Abbotsbury Abbey in about the 12th century. Now the site is a nature reserve and the Swans live freely in a wild state. They are provided with

nest material and the cygnets are carefully protected in order to maintain or increase the numbers nesting.

The Swan has been widely used in heraldry, and is often represented in its beautiful intimidatory display, its wings half raised above its back in a pleasing symmetrical arch, beneath which its neck is drawn right back. Here, peeping out from under the arch can sometimes be seen the heads of very young cygnets, bundles of grey down. Both parents take charge of the young, and are then much less mute, often uttering series of soft, low, plaintive notes, contact-keeping calls and gentle instructions to the family. They will hiss menacingly at man and his dog or any too daring intruder.

In full flight, the wings produce a rather pleasing lisping whistle with each beat and a flight of more than two or three together produces a rushing sound, as of angels in a hurry. Taking off from the water produces considerable disturbance for all around as the great bird thrashes the river with its wings, slapping its way with its feet over the water in rapid running steps until it is airborne. The runway may sometimes cover a stretch of 50m or more if there is no wind and woe to anything in the take-off path not quick enough to dive or make an escape. They will chase off intruders in the same way but without intending to take off, and before the next breeding season the cygnets will discover that they themselves have become intruders — understandably they take their rejection only slowly. However, their turn will come, though they will not breed until they are 2-3 years old.

Protection of the Swan goes back to before the 15th century, but purely on behalf of the Royal Family and those few whom Majesty might wish to reward with the privilege of owning their own Swans — any grabbing or poaching by others was punishable by both imprisonment and a fine. Roast Swan was a prestigious dish to serve up at a feast and the freedom to do so was jealously guarded.

Royal Swans were identified by nicking their bills. They were caught during a boating function known as Swan-upping, which took place annually when the young of the year were fully grown. The royal cipher was three nicks, and there were two nicks for a nobleman. Pubs often took their name or their inn sign from the heraldic figures of their noble owner, and this gave rise to the pub name, still met with earlier this century, of 'The Swan with Two Necks' — a (joking) corruption of 'two nicks'. Swan-upping is still carried out from London Bridge to Henley, Reading and Wallingford on the Thames.

There have been three mistaken beliefs about the Mute Swan, apart from the belief that it is mute. Firstly, it was thought that a blow in anger from one of its wings would break a man's leg; most unlikely except as the result of an ensuing fall, although it might well crack a child's bone.

Secondly, it was once believed that Swans lived for an extravagant number of years. The sober and eminent naturalists Willoughby and Ray, in their classic book of 1676, state that "It is a very long-lived fowl, so that it is thought to attain the age of three hundred years.". It can live to the good old age of 30 years, as ringed individuals have shown, but anything much above that must be quite uncommon, and triple centenarians a matter of dreams. It is true that the larger a bird is, the longer it may live, but this is a matter of physiology.

The most romantic mistaken belief was that the Swan sings just before death, a supposition that Plato, Aristotle and others accepted. Sadly, for it is tempting to think that this magnificent bird must herald its departure into the unknown in some idealised and pleasing way, there is, of course, no grain of truth in the story, the origin of which is quite unknown. But the thought that this regal being devotes its last breaths to a sad musical farewell has caught the imagination of poets and composers all down the ages.

Birds in August

Rook *Corvus frugilegus*

I saw the spiders marching through air,
Swimming from tree to tree that midewed day
In latter August when the hay came creaking to the barn

Robert Lowell, *Mr Edwards and the Spider*.

UGUST is the month for our adult summer visitors, wearied by bringing up one or more broods of young, to give absolute priority to their own condition, to get fit for the long journey south to escape our winter. Those that stay need to fatten up as well, though less urgently, to be ready for any unusual severities of the coming months. Birds often arrive across the North Sea from Scandinavia exhausted by strong head-winds. Many have been caught, weighed, ringed and released, and sometimes retrapped later at the same site, when it has been found that gains of up to 40% of their initial body weight have been made within perhaps a mere 3-5 days. This is the equivalent of a 12-stone man gaining nearly five stone in perhaps three to five weeks.

Fat is laid down in special areas, in particular on membranes inside the abdomen and in layers under the skin, just as it is in ourselves. The bird, however, needs it as fuel, an essential asset, not a handicap as in the 15-stone man, and burns it up while surviving long hours migrating without rest or opportunity to re-fuel, or through days of starvation in hard winters.

Much of the food eaten in the earliest part of this recuperation period goes into the creation of new feathers, a process expensive of energy. Summer wear and tear has been considerable and all the flight and body feathers, the former in particular, generally need replacing. The moult process is a complicated one, which varies from one group of birds to another. In some the process is gradual, perhaps one feather of each wing symmetrically at a time. A close look at a Rook at about this time of year as it flies overhead will show a symmetrical gap in the two outspread wings where a flight feather has been shed and the new feather not yet re-grown. The new feathers are still sprouting and are "in sheath", growing from follicles in the bird's skin; these continue to produce new feathers all the bird's life, the sprouts appearing in plastic like sheaths jutting from the skin. The old feathers are shoved out, rather as old milk teeth are given the push in youngsters by their second set. The process is under the control of hormones, but a 'fright moult' occurs on rare occasions in a terrified bird, involving the loss of a great bunch of feathers from certain parts of the body — an unhappy state of affairs, but possibly with a life-saving role.

The Blackbird, like many other birds, moults only some flight feathers in its first autumn (i.e. before it is a year old), and the remainder the following autumn. This can be readily recognised in the male Blackbird; in the first few weeks after fledging it is not black, but a deep brown, including the flight feathers. These latter, i.e. the primaries and secondaries, are not moulted until the bird is over a year old, and their chocolate brown colour is easily detected in the wing in comparison with the gleaming black of the rest of its new plumage. Thus the Blackbird running across your lawn can be recognised as having been born last summer and possibly in the garden itself. Have a look.

A totally different system applies in the ducks and geese, for they moult all their flight feathers at once and become completely flightless while the new feathers are growing, a process that may take 3-4 weeks before the new wings are capable of lifting the bird into the air in flight. Advantage has been taken of this vulnerable position, not only by natural predators, but by man, for food in primitive communities, but more especially today to discover more about the life and times of individuals. Sir Peter Scott was an initiator of expeditions to Iceland and other breeding grounds of wild geese to coincide with the time the birds were flightless. Over the years many hundreds were carefully herded, protesting loudly, into pens and given individually identifiable rings or wing-tags, some of which could be read at a distance through binoculars. The recovery of ringed birds shot by wildfowlers, or birds retrapped with nets on their winter feeding grounds in Britain or during another year's expedition back at their breeding grounds (sometimes years later, so harmless was the ringing procedure), has produced much new information. The work, indeed, was a great source of exact knowledge as to the movements and length of life of different species of wild geese, leading to much greater understanding of their lifestyle and the better evaluation of measures for their future protection. An important point to be made about research on birds is that its major object often is to discover how they can be helped to survive the pressures that modern civilisation is forcing on them and their habitats. Their care and safety is a paramount consideration in the setting up of any investigations into their lives and living ways.

The Song Thrush

That's the wise thrush; he sings each song twice over,
Lest you should think he never could recapture
The first fine careless rapture

Robert Browning, *Home Thoughts from Abroad.*

HE SONG THRUSH *Turdus philomelos* used to be one of our most familiar garden birds, present all the year and throughout the country, in many places commoner than the Blackbird. Today in many places it is a friendly surprise to see even one in the garden. The reasons for this tremendous change are not at all clear. Certainly the bird is a poor survivor in bad winters and has hardly adapted at all (as has the Blackbird) to accepting food put out by well-wishers during frosty weather. One can sometimes watch a Song Thrush hopping about on the ground surrounded by food that Blackbirds, tits and finches are gobbling up, apparently unable to recognise as food the bread and crumbs, peanuts and fat on offer. The Scilly Isles are a happy exception to this; Song Thrushes there are common, especially round picnic tables, and help themselves to your sandwich without a qualm. Importantly, it is now realised that the use of poisons in gardens against slugs, snails and worms, the Song Thrush's staple foods, is at least partly to blame for the catastrophic decline in numbers. The disuse of pest controls in the garden is strongly recommended unless you are certain they are harmless to other creatures besides the one that is annoying you.

The Thrush, as it is usually called, is a dapper, upright, clean-looking bird, warm brown above and creamy-white below, with conspicuous lines of clearcut, brown lozenge-shaped spots, mainly on the breast. The Mistle Thrush is larger, with bigger spots, more randomly scattered. But if you see a thrush with white tips to the outer tail feathers as it flies away from you (not difficult to pick up), then it is a Mistle Thrush. If it has a reddish patch showing on the flank, more obvious when it flies, and a pale line above the eye, then it is a Redwing, a common winter visitor, which only comes to gardens in hard weather. It is an enjoyable diversion looking for these features and successfully making the distinctions.

Snails are a staple food of Thrushes. They use 'anvils', favourite stones or hard flat surfaces, on which to hammer the snail, lifting it repeatedly in its beak and then bringing it down with a brutal whack on the hard surface, until enough shell has been dislodged for it to be able to extract the snail whole, then to wipe it on the ground before swallowing it. Where both Thrushes and snails are still common, such as in the Scilly Isles, this is quite a common sight, and one can watch from close range, so absorbed is the bird on the job in hand. It is not uncommon too to see a Thrush tugging at a partly embedded earthworm, legs braced back, head up and retracted, the poor worm stretching out as long as it can hold onto its burrow. Intriguing though the battle is, it is not conducive to *bon appetit* when viewed through the window while eating one's breakfast. Better enjoyment is had from watching the bird scrabbling about in leaf litter like a farmyard hen, looking for grubs and insects.

One hundred years ago, Alfred Newton, Professor of Zoology at Cambridge, a very eminent international leader in ornithology, described the Thrush as "very common", and in his well known *A Dictionary of Birds*, unashamedly says that its flesh was "justly esteemed for the table". In 1895, Heinrich Gätke wrote a major work, *Heligoland. An Ornithological Observatory*, a deservedly renowned and pioneering study of the day to day fluctuations in the number and species of birds on this small isolated island off the west coast of Germany. His records revealed for the first time that astonishing numbers of birds were on passage in autumn across the North Sea from the rest of northern Europe on their way south into southern Europe and Africa, with a smaller, but still spectacular, northern passage in spring. Like Newton, he too spoke of myriads of 'Throstles' and of "the pleasure of its highly agreeable taste . . second to none of the whole pack of its relatives". Expanding on this theme, he continues: ". . when the menu of the Heligolander's housewife contains the item *Troossel-supp* . . we may reckon with safety on the timely appearance of paterfamilias at the dinner table, his spoon held in readiness, and his mouth watering in expectation of the good things to come." Gätke implies too that he himself has this "epicurean weakness" and advises "everyone who catches the bird in sufficient numbers" not to roast them, "but, by way of trial, to confide some forty or fifty, according to requirements, to the soup pot". Both Gätke and Newton, it must be realised, were scholarly and highly motivated scientists who wished the study of ornithology to prosper. Their attitude was normal for the days when bird numbers were perhaps 100 times larger than today. It can be only in retrospect that their failure to recognise that condoning such habits and traditions would inevitably in time, together with other equally unrecognised factors, lead to the destruction of much that they held dear. We are not more righteous today, indeed less so, since we are so much better informed. One has only to compare the number of birds to be seen today with those of even 30 years ago to recognise that unrestricted so-called 'hunting' is inexcusable. In southern Western Europe and throughout the Mediterranean, up to 8 or 10 million — yes million — small migrant birds, not to mention tens of thousands of birds of prey, are slaughtered every year in the name of 'sport' or 'hunting' or for commercial gain. These numbers are far in excess of any slaughter that took place towards the end of the last century. Such insouciant disregard of the overwhelming evidence for possible extinctions ahead is unforgivable today and calls for ever increased vigilance on the part of conservation bodies and stricter controls of 'traditional hunting' by all governments.

On a lighter note, in the surprising world of ancient folklore, one J.Jonston stated that the Thrush was deaf, perhaps a misinterpretation of the attitude which a Thrush often adopts when prospecting a lawn for food, its head turned on one side the better to identify by sight, not hearing, a glimpse of movement from some poor worm. Also in the 17th century it was believed by some that when a Thrush was about ten years old, it lost both its legs and grew new ones. Would that we could all do so at an equivalent age, for ten is elderly indeed for a Thrush.

Birds in September

Dunlin *Calidris alpina*

Down the way Persephone goes,
just now, in first-frosted September

D.H. Lawrence, *Bavarian Gentians*.

EPTEMBER is a month in which there is much movement of birds to and from Britain. Our summer visitors, the warblers and others, set off across the Channel and the Bay of Biscay to France, Spain, North Africa and beyond; birds which have bred in Scandinavia cross the North Sea on their way south to or through Europe or North Africa; yet other migrants come over from the Low Countries and further east to our east and south-east counties, thence to spread across the country on their way to warmer climes. Still more movements come from the first of the winter visitors to arrive in Britain, such as the Redwing and Fieldfare, and all through the month the coastal areas of mudflats and marshland will be witnessing a constantly changing population of the wading birds, like Dunlin, Curlew Sandpiper, Whimbrel and Curlew, some of which may have bred as far north as the Arctic Circle. The population of our island is indeed a constantly changing and cosmopolitan one this month.

These tens of thousands of birds depend for their navigation on sight of the land, or of the sun, and in the case of nearly all the small perching birds, the night sky, since they travel all their main distances in the darkness of night, utilising the star patterns to maintain their course and their cries and contact calls to keep a group together. Thus it is that a flock of birds may be heard overhead and if the sky is so overcast that the birds cannot see the stars to guide them, they must rely on landmarks and guess-work to continue on the right track. However, if there is a strong wind blowing and they can see no land below them nor stars above, they will tend to fly downwind, thus using less energy, though the risk of finding themselves blown unwittingly out to sea is thereby magnified.

It has been shown by radar that most small birds travel mostly at 2,000-5,000ft, but larger species, like cranes and geese, can go to much greater heights, even up to 25,000ft or more, for example over the Himalayas. Other species that travel by day, such as Swallows, fly at much lower levels, feeding on airborne insects as opportunity offers. Night travellers held up by adverse weather and contrary winds may eventually give up waiting and set out in daylight. Streams of Skylarks have been watched flying in from the North Sea coast up the Firth of Forth against a strong westerly wind which had persisted for several days.

In the mid 19th century, for many decades the German naturalist Heinrich Gätke recorded the species and numbers from his house on Heligoland. An observatory was established in 1909 and large-scale trapping and ringing was instituted. Gätke used large, high walled, wire traps, open mouthed, roofed and tapering through several metres to a small box with a glass window at the farthest and smallest end, into which birds could be driven. These were given the name of 'Heligoland traps' and were used extensively later all over the Continent and British Isles, but mainly only since the end of the Second World War. Prior to those years there were only two such observatories in the UK — one on the Isle of May in the Firth of Forth and the other on the island of Skokholm off the Pembroke coast. There are now some 14 Bird Observatories manned most of the year, from Portland on the south coast near Weymouth to Fair Isle off Shetland in the far north, and from Lundy in the Bristol Channel to Gibraltar Point on the Wash in Lincolnshire. Cape Clear in southern Ireland is famous for its records of seabird migration. There are besides many bird observatories throughout Europe, the most famous being Rybachi in what used to be East Prussia, when it was known as Rossitten, Ottenby and Falsterbo in southern Sweden, the latter renowned for huge numbers of raptors — all of these on the Baltic coasts. A well recognised hazard for migrating birds, and one which is in many places now provided against, occurs on misty nights when birds find themselves attracted to the beams of a lighthouse, for instance on Heligoland or the Isle of May. Hundreds, sometimes thousands, may mill around for hours in the mist-filled beams, like moths round a lamp, many of them blindly dashing themselves against the lighthouse glass and falling dead or injured onto the lighthouse's gallery or into a merciless sea. At least some of those that perish so unhappily provide welcome evidence of the species travelling that night and, if they have been ringed, information from where they set out.

Garden Birds

Seen from the sitting room

The espaliers and the standards all
Are thine; the range of lawn park

Tennyson, *The Blackbird*.

E WAS SMALL and creeping along by the edge of the wall, busily peering here and there, gradually advancing along its length, apparently intent on keeping as near out of sight as possible. He hadn't noticed that rather behind him and out in the open was a larger alert individual moving in the same direction, eyes bright and sharply aware. They met at the end of the flower bed. Startled by the sudden presence of the other, the Wren immediately flew up into a rose bush and poured out his song at its most powerful, just as Wrens often do when startled, while the Blackbird flew off *chuk-chuk-chukking* noisily in High Dudgeon.

This little commotion seemed to be the cue for the garden brigand to enter, arriving with a great plomp in the middle of the small lawn, bouncing forward with the impetus of his sudden descent from the nearby pine trees, where he has his nest. He is a villain, the Magpie, but he is very smart in more ways than one. Imagine a tall well proportioned macho fellow, bedecked in tailor-made, expensive, smart blue-black and white morning tails of an unusual cut, with a proud, upright bearing, a bright eye and complete self-confidence, a rival for any Georgian dandy — and there is the strutting Magpie. If only he wasn't such a skilled plunderer of his smaller neighbours' eggs and young and would confine himself to scavenging, what a blameless pleasure his handsome presence would be in any garden.

Over at the bird-bath, carefully placed at ground level, is a good friend. However, he has a habit in bad taste of crooning an oft repeated pronouncement about the listener's very personal internal habits, which are none of his concern anyhow — *Your bowels ache, Your bowels ache.* This is the Collared Dove and some there are who find his frequent admonishments a real trial on a hot summer day in the garden. But they are lovely, the pair usually together, both prettily adorned in similar delicate greys and pale browns. As a suitor, the male has a charming court-ship flight, first flying upwards quite slowly to near tree top level, continuing with motionless wide-spread wings on an upward climb, which arches into a gentle downward glide, wings still spread for a few more seconds before flying off to a perch or sweeping up again to repeat these graceful movements. One can be nearly sure that the focus of his attentions is taking notice.

A later look finds Willie, the Pied Wagtail, sprinting across the grass in quick dashes, picking off tiny midges, flies and other insects, until after a lively short while it has a satisfying beakfull of untidy wings and pieces and abruptly takes off, flying purposefully towards its nest full of young. An exemplary father, or indeed mother for that matter, since the two closely resemble each other, he is *Motacilla alba*; there is a West African cousin whose second name is the odd one of *aguimp*, a native name from Namibia, appropriately meaning 'field or beach runner'.

Over at the back of the garden, and walking ploddingly this way is the stout body of a Woodpigeon, on his way to the bird bath for a drink. Doves and pigeons drink in a way different from most of our other birds. They favour the beer drinkers' habit, sticking their beak into the water, sucking deeply and swallowing without raising the head at all (unless alarmed) until the crop is full or they are out of breath. All the other garden birds are the lager sippers, dipping down to the water to take a beakfull, to be swallowed only when the head is raised and thrown back. Shy, evasive birds like Woodpigeons and Magpies have recently changed character remarkedly and are now very much at home in many gardens, though in suburban gardens the Woodpigeon has often been much more confiding than in the country. On one occasion, in Hampstead, a pair had nested on an open horizontal branch of a large Beech tree in a back garden. Imagine the horror of children finding a hideous, half naked, fairly well grown squab, as the nestlings are called, on the ground under the nest. But rescue was at hand — a rope was thrown over the branch, some 25ft up, a small basket attached to one end, into which the squab was packed, apparently content with the attention it was getting. With great care the basket was hoisted until it reached the edge of the branch, when to everyone's surprised gratification the squab immediately scrambled out and almost trotted along the branch to join its sibling in the nest 2ft away.

These garden Woodpigeons used to be greatly disliked for greedily demolishing precious greens and broccoli, but now, of course, it is illegal to shoot within 50ft of a public way, and for another thing, neighbours rightly do not tolerate slaughter amongst the flower beds. The Sparrow-hawk has also benefited from this change in law and order, and may be quite a menace hedge-hopping along a row of back gardens, surprising the small birds tamely feeding at the bird tables, ruthlessly picking off one of them with its long legs, to devour it in some secluded corner nearby.

The make up of our garden birds is changing all the time, and sadly these days their numbers and variety continue gradually to decline. We still have our Robins, Blackbirds, tit families, Nuthatches, Song and Mistle Thrushes, Dunnocks, warblers, Collared Doves, Chaffinches and Greenfinches, maybe Goldfinches, Swallows and House Martins and even Goldcrests; but it is imperative that we take care of them, avoid poisoning them, discourage our cats from catching the unwary fledglings, provide them with suitable food in winter and nest-sites in spring, water to drink and bathe in all the year. We must do this positively if we are to continue to enjoy their company.

The Collared Dove

For years fleet away with the wings of the dove

Byron, *The First Kisses of Love*.

HE COLLARED DOVE *Streptopelia decaocto* loves parks and farmyards, is a regular marauder of chicken runs, and, of course, is a familiar garden bird. It selects and profits by the neighbourhood of Man, feeding contentedly on seeds and spilt grain, sensibly mostly avoiding city centres and heavily built up and polluted areas. The plumage is a soft 'dove' grey, its only prominent feature being the white showing on the upper part of the spread wing; there is white also at the tips of the underside of its tail feathers, contrasting with the black bases, quite conspicuous when it swoops up onto a perch. At rest, the black half collar at the side of the neck is easily seen and gives the bird its name. However, its rather monotonous call is what attracts (or distracts) one's attention most, *coo coo coo*, with the emphasis on the second syllable. Its conversation has been translated in many personal ways, some quite bizarre.

Familiar though it now is, no wild Collared Dove was seen anywhere in this country until 1952. Today it breeds throughout the British Isles. Indeed, its distribution in Europe before 1930 was only well to the east, being confined to Turkey and small parts of the eastern Balkans. About that time it started expanding its range northwestwards with unexampled rapidity, invading Europe through Hungary, Czechoslovakia, Austria and Germany, to reach the North Sea in Holland in 1947 and Denmark the next year, followed by Switzerland, Sweden, France, Belgium and Norway by 1952, all countries where it had never been seen before. This was an extension of its range by some 1,000 miles in less than 20 years, an explosive and quite exceptional rate of spread for any bird. So it was not surprising that several writers by then had forecast its imminent arrival in England. In May 1952 one was seen and heard almost exactly where predicted, in Lincolnshire. No-one, however, predicted that this expansion would continue much further, into the inhospitable north, yet by 1970 it had indeed reached the Faeroes and Iceland. This remarkable expansion has been due almost certainly to the Collared Dove 'discovering' and then filling a habitat niche which was unoccupied by any other bird of competitive or similar size, with like feeding habits. Thus blessed with few or no adversaries, it had to expand its range to accommodate the resulting great increase in numbers. The spread was undoubtedly aided by its confiding adaptability to Man's unintentional bounty in supplying spilt grain, together with its own zest for breeding, sometimes resulting in four broods in one year. No more than two eggs are laid in a clutch, and those on a flimsy mattress of bare dead twigs, often horribly exposed and accessible to such villains as Squirrels, Magpies and Jackdaws — yet its numbers must have increased by millions in the past 50 years.

James Fisher, who did so much in pre-television years to popularise natural history by thought-provoking programmes on radio, proclaimed birdwatching to be not only an interesting pursuit in itself, but one with scientific usefulness. It was he who had predicted the Collared Dove's arrival on the Lincolnshire coast to within a few miles where it was found by his friend, Reg May, a Lincolnshire postman and brilliant field observer. Later James Fisher wrote up the details of this population explosion. He starts his account by quoting an ancient Greek legend recounted by a naturalist, one C. Hinke, in 1837:

> "A poor maid was servant to a very hard-hearted lady, who gave her as wages no more than 18 pieces a year. The maid prayed to the Gods that she would like it to be made known to the world how miserably she was paid by her mistress. Thereupon Zeus created this Dove, which proclaims an audible *deca-octo* [= 18] to all the world to this very day."

Even if the dove's call was interpreted with imaginative licence by Zeus, his creation and this legend sufficiently intrigued a Hungarian ornithologist, one Frivaldskzy, who was the first to describe the species in 1838, to give it the specific name *deca-octo*, and so it has, indeed, remained ever since. It is a charming bird and one for which one may indulge one's own fancies to provide a fairy tale explanation of its name and its notable, inoffensive invasion of western Europe.

Birds in October

Waxwing *Bombycilla garrulus*

Listen! the wind is rising,
and the air is wild with leaves;
We have had our summer evenings,
now for October eves!

Humbert Wolfe, *Autumn*.

Y THE END of this month many of the visitors from northern Europe and Scandinavia will have arrived and spread across the country, escaping from the oncoming cold and very short days of the near-Arctic. On the coasts, the mudflats and marshlands will be occupied by hosts of waders, which have to feed continuously to maintain their body weight or to increase it, if like many of them they are only in transit in the British Isles, on their way to the Mediterranean and North and West African coasts. In many areas feeding opportunity is at the bidding of the tide, which may flow in to cover all the mud on which the birds depend for the worms, molluscs and crustacea which it contains. At places like Hilbre Island in the Dee estuary, birds are numbered at times in hundreds of thousands. At high tide they are compressed into the island's tiny space because the 60 or so square miles of the estuary are covered in water. The different species huddle together in great packs, shoulder to shoulder, restless or fitfully sleeping, keeping up an apparently never ending conversation, the Oystercatchers *pipping*, godwits grunting, gulls yelling, and the small waders like Dunlin twittering on and on; now and again comes the lovely evocative cry of the Curlew "bewailing its long nose" as T.H. White writes.

Towards the end of the month and onwards into the winter bad weather and the shortage of their preferred or essential foods may bring over the North Sea less common and irregular visitors, such as the Crossbill, the Waxwing, aptly named for the little red wax-like tips to a few feathers on the wing and Arctic Redpolls *Carduelis hornemanni*, which breed as far north as 80°N, unlike our Redpolls *Carduelis flammea* which breed in East Anglia, in the north of the British Isles, Wales and western Ireland. Nutcrackers, more at home in the pine forests and snows of the mountains of central eastern Europe very occasionally appear. In some years numbers are exceptional and their arrival, probably over a matter of only a week or two, is a real irruption. These species, though a few may arrive every year in the British Isles, are adapted to live in the cold winters of the north and of central Europe. But when weather conditions are even more severe than usual and the seed supply from the pine forests fails, or the lemming and other small mammal populations are minimal, flocks of poorly nourished birds will be forced to move into more temperate areas and irrupt onto the East coast of England, while others such as the Snowy Owl and Gyrfalcon come south in ones and twos to northern Scotland. Some irruptions are harder to explain. Pallas's Sandgrouse, plump and partridge like and about the same size, had hardly ever occurred in England, being an inhabitant of central Asia, until 1863 when many small flocks reached into different areas of the country, as far south-west as the Scillies, and west into Ireland and north-west to the Outer Hebrides. In another irruption a quarter of a century later in May 1888, a pair even nested in Yorkshire. Small invasions have occurred on about nine occasions since then, but since 1911 there has been but one record. An unusual and unexplained history.

Meanwhile and closer to home, our common garden birds have settled into their winter home areas. Most of them lead a comparatively unaggressive life, content to live and let live. The Robin, by now will have established a winter territory, and most unusually both the males and females stake out claims in active rivalry. Even more exceptionally, the female Robin, silent all the rest of the year, sings as heartily as the male, and with the same song, though the winter song is noticeably different from the male's musical tinkling of the spring and summer. The tits will be seen in small parties, probably one or more families together, doing their rounds of the newly furbished bird-tables. The garden Blackbirds tend to stay in the same areas which they occupied in the summer, but the summer bonds between a pair are no more permanent than they so often are amongst ourselves.

Our Chaffinches are quite sedentary and have seldom been found to move more than 5-20km away from where they were born. The flocks that appear at the edges of woods and in stubble fields are of immigrants from Europe and Scandinavia, and with them may be one or two male Bramblings, handsome in their bold orange waistcoats and black mantles. Greenfinches may wander away further from home, but only in the nature of a dispersal, there is no suggestion of migration. There are of course winter flocks, as with the Chaffinch, but they also are of immigrants from Europe and the north. These flocks will not be very conspicuous until the end of the month. Rooks and Jackdaws are in flocks, and can be seen collecting to go off to roost together, though the Jackdaws will still return often to the chimneys where they were born or bred. October seems to have rather the air of a waiting time, and though there can be grand spells of sunny warmth, 'Indian summers', autumn is coming to an end. Winter is on its way and preparations must be made and habits changed to suit. We too should take note.

≈ The Starling ≈

The Starling claps his tiny castanets

Tennyson

TARLING is the diminutive of the early English *Stare* and the adult bird and all its relatives are now known by that name. The Starling *Sturnus vulgaris* was a bird well recognised and observed by the ancients, who were particularly struck by its considerable ability to mimic. Pliny, that great fount of knowledge, alludes to it as "trained for the amusement of the young Caesars . . . [and] capable of uttering both Latin and Greek", which is more than can be said in general for the modern schoolboy.

In the early days of radar, when unexplained images on the screen were entertainingly referred to as Angels, one occasional early morning phenomenon was the sudden appearance of expanding rings, like those made by a fish rising to a fly on the surface of still water, where nothing had been visible just before. Some pundits explained it in learned meteorological terms, since the idea that birds, even in flocks, could produce such images was given little or no credence. But these particular Angels were shown to be explosive departures of hosts of Starlings from large roosts, which they form in autumn and winter. Sometimes these are made up of hundreds of thousands of birds, and indeed on occasion over a million have been estimated to occupy a single roost. Owners of woodland find such multitudes most unwelcome; hundreds of trees may be overwhelmed in but a few weeks by the sheer weight of such legions and by the great mass of droppings. The birds' sudden departure en masse in early morning from such sites shows up fleetingly on the radar as rings expanding outwards from the roost, until the crowding together of the birds diminishes sufficiently to throw no shadow. Weather whims and quirks have no connection at all.

The Starling is a most successful species, a survivor. Its natural range is northern Europe and Asia, but it has been unwisely introduced to several countries, sometimes deliberately by sentimental immigrants missing the "old country", or unknowingly by ships; and it is now spreading widely in North America, southern Africa, Australia and New Zealand, in some cases at the expense of native species.

Hyperactive, busy and bustling, the Starling is also strong and aggressive, as can too often be seen at garden bird tables. One very eminent character is known to have attached to his bird table an electric bell which he could actuate from his sitting room armchair to frighten off these gobblers of feasts intended for quite other and more agreeable birds.

Nesting in holes in trees, or in slits such as are found under the eaves of houses, at any height, it has few enemies, especially in suburbia, and indeed suffers most molestation at nesting times from its own kind seeking to take over a nest site, young and eggs being flung out indiscriminately. Since it usually has two broods and lays 4-5 eggs each time, it might be expected to spread widely; and indeed its numbers were steadily increasing over the 100 years or more up to the 1960s. Since then, however, there has been an unexplained decline in numbers, most noticeably of the migrants that take refuge here from the bitter winters of northeastern Europe. The British Isles has its own resident population, but late autumn brings in large flocks from the north and east, though their total numbers have been fewer in the last 20 years, perhaps due to unrevealed disasters in west and central Asia. Could radio-active leaks or contaminated clouds be a likely cause?

The Starling feeding on your lawn may be taking food off the surface, but most often it is probing the ground for insects and larvae. The closed bill is inserted into the soil, and then opened to make a hole, down which it peers, swivelling its eyes forwards so that it has binocular vision, instead of its usual separate-eyed sideways views. Not only that but the eyes can be rotated up and back while the head is still bent forwards so that the bird can keep an eye literally open to spot danger from behind and above. All this is an interesting evolution that has required recognisable modifications to the relevant muscles and to the skull bones to which they are attached.

For all its aggressive and rather brash behaviour, the Starling has many enjoyable features. Watch him or her on a bright spring day of full sunshine, stationed on a telephone wire, and if the angle of the sunlight is right, the usually dull-looking blackish plumage becomes transformed into one showing iridescent greens and purples, a faint copy of its tropical relatives, the Glossy Starlings, which can always provide the loveliest shimmering of glinting blues and greens and purples. Enjoy too our bird perched, and with the greatest ardour, singing — creating a "medley of throaty warbling, chirruping, clicking, and gurgling sounds, interspersed with musical whistles and pervaded by a peculiar creaky quality", as it has been so well described. In addition the keen ear may recognise the mimicked phrase of more than one other species incorporated into what seems a slightly frantic performance, delivered with body upright and the long sharp pointed throat feathers puffed out. Seen thus, the Starling is to be admired as an enjoyable comic, and one can forgive him that sometimes he can be a bit of a selfish bully.

The Long-tailed Tit

HE LONG-TAILED TIT belongs to a different genus (*Aegithalos*) from all the other common tits of the garden (*Parus*), and indeed they are considered nowadays to be of different families. Busy, agile and acrobatic like the other tits, they are more tiny, only 8-9gm in weight, and daintily water-coloured in pink and grey and black. The tail really is long, longer than the body, black, with the outermost feathers conspicuously white. Except when they are nesting, they go about in family parties, softly chittering to keep in touch as they go. Several will be seen together in a low tree restlessly searching for food, and at intervals individuals will dart off to the next hunting ground, perhaps a tall bush only a few yards away. Sometimes the whole party may take off together, and will then be seen flitting across a gap in bouncing flight, occasionally in line astern. Their behaviour is a delight, and their appearance charming, especially as they have the rather chubby, foreshortened innocent face associated with young animals, enhanced by a pink tummy and a similar pink patch on the shoulders.

The Long-tailed Tit of Great Britain is a race or subspecies which is endemic to these islands, i.e. it is slightly different from those in other countries and does not occur anywhere else. Across the Channel, features change, though the visual differences are small — and thankfully there is no change in character, language or charm.

Unlike the common garden tits, the Long-tailed Tit does not nest in a hole, but creates, so to speak, its own in the form of a domed nest. This is a prettily and cleverly constructed home, about the size and shape of an Ostrich's egg or a generous Easter egg, created entirely of cob-webs, hair and the tiniest fragments of moss, stuccoed on all sides with diminutive blobs of grey lichen, and so skilfully camouflaged that it is easily overlooked. On the other hand the pair takes few pains to hide its building activities, which can sometimes be watched openly from as close as 3m. The process is fascinating. A cup is first formed, in a small fork of, say, a Silver Birch tree or in a tangle of wild rose. Both birds keep at it individually for many hours daily for a week or more. Arriving with a tiny piece of material, the builder sits in the cup it has first made, its tail raised comically over its back, and places its load on the outside of the rim. This addition, perhaps threads of cobweb, is then pulled over the top of the rim from the outside, and tucked painstakingly into the inside. Both birds enter the cup at the same point on the rim, and this ends up as the entrance hole to the nest. When the cup sides have grown quite tall, build-ing is continued just on the far side. The elongated, elevated wall which results eventually forms the dome. The bird sits inside the cup as before, but has to lean its neck out over its back to pull this roof over to join the wall on which it is sitting. Much forceful shoving and shoring up from inside is needed. The whole internal shape of this bijou residence is created by the builder sitting and shifting round and round in the cup as it grows, moulding it to the shape and size of its body and, of course, accommodating its long tail over its back. Finally a lining of tiny downy feathers is installed to make comfortable the 8-10 eggs that will be laid.

Diligent people have counted these lining feathers and report that on average there are some 1,550 to each nest. It has also been shown that feathers may be fetched from as far away as 200 yards. But even if the average distance is only 30 yards the total distance travelled by the pair is over 25 miles. What labour!

A common name in Oxfordshire and Berkshire for the Long-tailed Tit used to be Bottle Tit, not for any obvious reason today. But there are many other rather obscure country names. Feather Poke is understandable, as is Oven Bird, or even Fluffit; but Bum Barrel and Bum Towel need a deal of imagination to explain. It is probable that the words used have over the years changed their meaning, resting as they do on information from the middle of the last century. A 'bum' for instance, as well as its schoolboy meaning, can mean a sponger, a loafer or mean fellow, or it can refer to a bee's hum. But in today's parlance none of these names seems appropriate for our alert, pretty and attractive Long-tailed Tit.

Birds in November

Wren Troglodytes troglodytes

November's sky is chill and drear,
November's leaf is red and sear.

Walter Scott, *Marmion*.

OVEMBER is an unpleasant month, more often than not plagued by fogs and damp grey days. Birds must dislike it just as much as we do, since they only show themselves when venturing out of shelter to feed, when they must stoke up enough to survive the ordeal of damp or frosty nights. It is difficult not to feel helpless pity at the sight of a mite of a bird foraging late in oncoming night for the food essential to avoid hypothermia during the next 12 hours — out of doors in a heavy frost. Yet the fittest survive.

To add to November gloom, bird song is very subdued, though Song Thrushes, Robins, Wrens and Collared Doves may be heard. There are, too, calls of fright or warning, such as when a Blackbird, suddenly disturbed, panics away across the garden, squawking as it goes, or the aptly described 'scolding' of an upset Wren.

To escape from annual inclement or dangerous weather, birds have three main choices. Many of them migrate to warm climates. Many others have adapted to survive on a diet of what food remains available even in the harshest conditions of the far north, and when this fails, to move south to where the food is still plentiful. In some years birds such as Crossbills and

Waxwings, will suddenly appear in swarms from Scandinavia, when their sources of food have started to run out.

The third alternative is torpidity or hibernation, not one that is usually associated with birds. There is one species, a desert nightjar of North America, unkindly called the Common Poorwill (its pathetic sounding name is related to its call), which hides in small rock crevices, remaining there in a state of torpidity for possibly several weeks during a very cold winter. Its temperature is then half that of normal, and without special apparatus its breathing and heart-beat cannot be detected at all. This dormancy or suspended animation resulting from a reduction in breathing and heart rate also occurs in some species of hummingbird; but this takes place only when they are roosting at night and when the air temperature is sharply reduced after the sun sets, mostly in high mountainous areas. Members of another family, the swifts, such as the White-throated Swift of California, resort to dormancy in certain freezing conditions at night, possibly for 2-3 days in exceptional conditions. Such methods of counteracting severe cold are not used by any British bird; indeed a prolonged heavy frost causes decimation in the numbers of many small species such as the Wren and Robin. Their only recourse is to hide away in some sheltered, unexposed corner, perhaps in a tree hole or deep in a thick matt of ivy and to use the insulating effect of the downy base of their body feathers as a duvet.

In his well-known book *The Natural History of Selborne* first published in December 1778, the Rev Gilbert White (in his church at Selborne there is a delightful modern stained glass window full of bird portraits, the Saint Francis window) showed great puzzlement, as did all naturalists of the time, as to how and where Swallows spent the winter :

> ". . I used to spend some weeks yearly at Sunbury, . . .near Hampton Court. In the autumn . . . .what struck me most was, that, from the time they [Swallows] began to congregate, forsaking the chimnies and houses, they roosted every night in the osier beds of the aits of the river. Now this resorting to this element, at that season of the year, seems to give some countenance to the northern opinion (strange as it is) of their retiring under water."

(In this context 'northern' referred to Scandinavia.) It seems extraordinary today that such an idea could be taken seriously, but there was scant belief that such "weak" creatures could possibly fly over great distances to Africa, where of course it was known that Swallows did occur. Naturalists were also confused by late and not necessarily correct identifications of Swallows in November and even December — they did not have any aids like binoculars, only their own eyes and ears, and of course the gun. It is easy to take a light-hearted view of such surmises that even a highly intelligent, wonderfully observant and well informed parson held 200 years ago, but should we not wonder whether we ourselves today are holding views on nature which are perhaps equally totally at odds with reality and will be recognised as such in another 200 years?

❧ The Heron ❧

My dreams are full of herons dancing in the mud.
Crazy dreams.

Bob Turpin, *Heron*.

HE COMMON or Grey Heron *Ardea cinerea* is a great lordly bird, serene and rather solitary, although it nests in colonies. Its long neck is white, with attractive black dashes in vertical lines adorning the front, its legs long and spindly, and its bill large and yellow. In flight, the long legs are extended out behind and its broad wings look cumbersome, their trailing half black; but the closed wing hides the black completely. A few black plumes stretch from behind the eye to well beyond the crown. The neck is straightened only when the bird is active on the ground; in flight or at rest it hunches its neck into an S-bend.

The Heron is shy and wary, placing no trust in Man — greatly adept at hiding itself at the river's edge or by some small stream or pond. It may roost or rest out in the middle of open meadows where it can command a wide field of view, and in icy weather may be seen anywhere where it can find food. Herons suffer badly in severe winters, their numbers decreasing dramatically during lengthy spells of frost.

The flight is slow and ponderous, yet at times a bird will suddenly 'wiffle'. This jolly antic is a way of returning suddenly to earth out of an apparently clear sky by side-slipping and zigzagging down at great speed to a safe and perfectly controlled landing — rather startling in such a large bird. Rooks quite often behave in the same way. It is difficult not to think that it is done purely for pleasure.

Our heron, 90cm in length, is of middling size in its family group of 35 herons and egrets, ranging from the 30cm (12ins) of the smallest, the tiny Zigzag Heron of South America with its wavy zebra-like markings, to the 140cm or 4.5ft of the aptly named Goliath Heron of Africa and south-west Asia with its gorgeous chestnut head, neck and belly.

Grey Herons breed almost invariably in colonies. Pennant, writing in the 1760s in his great work *British Zoology*, cites a huge heronry near Spalding in Lincolnshire in which one "spreading oak" contained not less than 80 nests. Incongruously for such an ungainly looking bird, the nests are placed for safety near the tops of trees. One almost holds one's breath watching a bird coming in to land, long legs dangling, broad wings frantically flapping, with apparently nowhere safe to set down without causing utter havoc over a wide area of the colony. Everything, nevertheless, is fully under control and a harmless landing is almost invariable. Squabbling, on the other hand, is much in evidence all the nesting season — indeed thieving and repeated unfaithfulness are probably rife.

Interestingly too, Pennant states that the great colony he cites gave him the "opportunity of detecting my own mistake.....in making two species of Heron". He and others had mistaken the Heron in its full breeding dress, "with its snowy neck and long crest streaming in the wind", for a separate species, the 'Crested Heron', a crest which it loses when the nesting season is over. In those days, of course, optical aids were negligible and most identifications were made from corpses. Field observation and recognition were only just beginning to be considered as an alternative to shooting. Pennant and his famous correspondent Gilbert White were almost the first to set store by keen attention to detail of the live wild bird. Nevertheless the dictum "What's hit is history; what's missed is mystery" holds sway even to this day amongst some doubting collectors. Field craft today requires detailed knowledge and acute observation; sightings of rarities only get into the record book after careful scrutiny by a body of experts.

One never ceases to be astonished by the observations of the ancients. Aristotle says in one passage on the Heron, which he calls Pella: "The coupling of the Pella is difficult, for it screams as it couples and (they say) emits blood from its eyes; it also brings forth painfully and with extreme distress." Srange observations, indeed, and clearly some imaginative interpretations.

In days long gone, the Heron was regularly eaten and in the 15th century one bird cost 16d, while four larks were 1d and a dozen thrushes cost 6d. Details of a gargantuan meal exist, provided for a feast to celebrate the Archbishop of York's enthronement in 1465: 400 'Heronshaws' were ordered, 2,000 geese, 104 Peacocks, 400 Swans, 4,000 ducks, in a total of over 16,000 birds, let alone 4,000 rabbits, fish, porpoises and seals, and of course roast domestic animals. The Lord Mayor's Banquet in the City of London is as nothing to this.

When hawking was at its most popular, the Heron was strictly protected on estates, since it provided a "marvellous and delectable pastime", as quarry for trained falcons. At a disadvantage in flight, the Heron was a good match for the hawk when brought to ground, and falconers would make haste to separate the antagonists before the Heron's long and very strong bill did mortal harm to their patiently trained and valuable birds.

Despite being so well known, the Heron has attracted little and dull folklore down the centuries. Perhaps the most unlikely tale comes once more from Ireland. This put forward the belief that small eels "pass through the Heron's intestines. . . uninjured, so that it swallows the same individual several times in succession". Clearly not a very sustaining diet, and one in which this wise and well adapted bird cannot really have indulged.

❧ Winter Birds ❧

Winter, tempest-robed,
In gloomy grandeur o'er the hills and seas
Reigneth omnipotent

Thomas Wade, *The Winter Shore*.

HE BIRDS you see in your garden in winter may be little, if any, different from the company you enjoy in the summer. Blue Tits and Great Tits come more often in early winter, since plenty of young born in the summer still survive the trials of hard weather and other dangers; but many of these youngsters will die before the spring, mainly through their lack of experience. Robins may also be more conspicuous, since both he and she defend and advertise by song the boundaries of his and her own winter homeland. But the Robin of today may not be the Robin which came gardening with you in the summer, indeed may even have come from outside the neighbourhood.

One winter visitor, a comparative newcomer to bird tables, is the Siskin, a rather small, quite smart-looking seed-eating finch, worth expecting. At a glance, the females and juveniles are greenish-yellow, with much brown streaking. The less often seen male is much more dapper. He has a yellow-green rump and yellow and black bands across the wing. A feature which distinguishes him from all other finches, is his black crown and tiny black chin. The Greenfinch is considerably larger and the yellow on the wing is along the edge of the wing, not across it. Away from the garden Siskins are tree-top birds, almost as acrobatic as tits, often found in silver birches and alders.

As winter drearily grows colder, food for birds becomes less easily found, and the bird table more popular. An appearance of the Great Spotted Woodpecker is always exciting, large and showy in black, white and red; but in reality he is a bully and drives everyone else away, even the trespassing squirrel. The Nuthatch is commoner and a more welcome visitor, usually approaching from out of the upper or middle branches of a tree, adroitly descending head first. The Treecreeper, rarely seen at the bird table, spirals up the trunk of a tree from the bottom, in search of tiny insects in the bark.

Only in the severest weather, when the main berry crops are all consumed and the fields deeply hardened by frost, do the Redwing and Fieldfare come to the garden. Winter visitors from the north, they are common country-wide, always in flocks and very talkative. They spread out over grassy fields, searching single-mindedly for earthworms, beetles and grubs, or occupy tall hedges, plucking and gulping berries, particularly hips and haws. The Redwing closely resembles our Song Thrush, but the Fieldfare is a much larger thrush, grey headed and grey rumped, with a chestnut back, rather good-looking.

Of our summer warblers, only some Blackcaps and Chiffchaffs may spend the winter here. The Blackcap quite often comes to a bird table, especially if currants or sultanas are on offer. Only the male Blackcap has a black crown, the female's being a rather fetching chestnut. Surprisingly, it has been found that the wintering Blackcaps are not our breeding birds, but from Germany and other central European countries. All of our warblers go south to the coasts of the Mediterranean and far beyond into Africa. Sadly they have first to run the gauntlet of the heartless, unthinking, so-called hunters of southern Europe and the Mediterranean, who continue to slaughter annually literally millions of not only their own but also everyone else's birds as they migrate through France, Spain, Italy and Mediterranean islands such as Malta, Cyprus and Crete. These countries have very deserving and active bird conservation societies, some with branches in this country, but their national protection laws are regularly ignored and the authorities mostly too frightened, personally or politically, to enforce them. Tradition, selfishness and ignorance die hard.

Interestingly, the Blue Tit you see today at your table may not be the one you saw yesterday, or even one of the same bunch you may think visit you throughout the winter. Over 100 have been caught and ringed in a single garden during one winter, many to be noticed in several other surrounding gardens later. Clearly a circuit is made of the neighbouring bird tables for weeks on end and one can develop a quiet self-satisfaction from watching from a nice warm room an ever varying throng of birds enjoying one's own generosity in providing bird food.

❧ December's Bird ❧

When winter frost
makes earth as steel
I search and search
But find no meal,
And most unhappy
Then I feel

Thomas Hardy, *The Robin.*

O CHRISTMAS is complete without a Robin. Brightly coloured and decorative, it is at home in your garden when few other birds show themselves. It appears in shop window displays, on the stage in panto-mimes, on wrapping paper and above all on Christmas cards. Friendly and confiding, essentially independent, naturally charming in behaviour, it is not easily roused, but becomes hostile and courageous in defence of its estate, home and family. It can sing most beautifully, sometimes sweetly *sotto voce*. So it has been for many centuries and so it will continue to be for centuries more.

Some Robins spend only the winter in Britain, having migrated south from Scandinavia, occasionally in spectacular numbers. In autumn 1951 there was a huge inrush of birds, including thousands of Robins, startling enough to have been reported in the national press. Evidently birds came together in huge numbers on the north coasts of the North Sea, prevented by the weather from migrating further, until one evening or night, conditions improving, waves of birds moved out to cross the unfriendly ocean. This happened on three successive nights, and late each night the weather must have turned against them, for on all three mornings tens of thousands of tired night migrating birds made coastal landfalls, from Fair Isle, near the Shetlands, south to the coast of Norfolk. At east coast bird observatories over 1,400 Robins were counted on 1 October, 500 or more at one observatory alone, with even more the next day. Imagine an influx one morning of hundreds of birds, including 500 Robins. in an area the size of a small village shopping centre! The Robins were not alone; there were many Thrushes and Blackbirds and, large numbers of the diminutive Goldcrest with them, an unforgettable spectacle for those lucky enough to have been present.

The Robin is known to everyone and many have had its name given to them — Robin Hood and Christopher Robin are perhaps two of the best known. Also the name has been given to several of the world's birds because of their red breasts, most notably the American Robin, which in fact is a large, rather ungainly looking member of the thrush family. Originally called Redbreast, then Robin Redbreast, and only in the last 150 years more consistently Robin, this endearing character is probably the first bird that a small child tries to draw. Its confiding nature and its chubby appearance, with puffed out feathers trying to keep warm in snowy weather, has made it the theme of many folk myths. Its slaughter, even so comparatively recently as just before the First World War, was regarded as sacrilege.

The origins of nearly all the superstitions and beliefs about the Robin are now lost in the mists of time. There was the legend that a Robin attempted to draw the nails from the cross and to pluck a thorn from the Crown of Thorns at the Crucifixion, and that a drop of blood falling on its breast during its compassionate endeavours gave the bird its gorgeous colouring. One of the most widespread traditions was that the Robin's wife was the Wren and there are many ancient simple rhymes referring to this unlikely belief. John Webster's lines in *The White Devil* were prompted by the belief that unburied bodies were at risk of ending up in limbo at the Second Coming :

> " Call for the redbreast and the wren,
> Since oe'r shady groves they hover,
> And with leaves and flowers do cover
> The friendless bodies of unburied men."

Many birds in this country have had mysteries attached to them, but where are such beliefs now? Superstitions, which are the basis of legends, have died out in the materialistic and sceptical outlook of today. They have mostly been the product of simple, unsophisticated but observant country folk, who needed their own explanations for apparently unusual behaviour. But the friendliness and confiding nature of the British Robin will continue to rouse, if not legends, certainly affection and interest into an indefinite future. Would that our British pride, today so obviously and unnecessarily lacking, could regain some of the Robin's enduring character. It is, after all, our National Bird.

Robin *Erithacus rubecula*, from *Illustrated Manual of British Birds*, 1889.

Works Consulted

APLIN, O.V. 1889. *The Birds of Oxfordshire*. Witherby.

BRUCKER, J.W., GOSLER, A.G. & HERYET, A.R. (Eds.) 1992 *Birds of Oxfordshire*. Pisces Publications.

BURY, J.B. 1886. Jynx in Greek Magic. *Journal of Hellenic Studies* 7:157.

CAMPBELL, B. & LACK, E. (Eds.) 1985. *A Dictionary of Birds*. T. & A.D.Poyser.

CLARK KENNEDY, A.W.M. 1868. *The Birds of Berkshire and Buckinghamshire*. Ingalton & Drake.

COOK, A.B. 1914. *Zeus*. London.

CRAMP, S. *et al.* (Eds.) 1977-1994. *Handbook of the Birds of Europe, the Middle East and North Africa*. Vols. I-IX Oxford University Press.

GÄTKE, H. 1895. *The Birds of Heligoland*. David Douglas.

HARTING, J.E. 1871. *The Birds of Shakespeare*. Van Voorst.

HOWARD, R, & MOORE, A. 1991. (2nd Edn.) *A Complete Checklist of the Birds of the World*. Academic Press.

HUME, R. 1990. *Birds by Character*. Papermac.

JOBLING, J.A. 1991. *A Dictionary of Scientific Bird Names*. Oxford University Press.

MONK, J.F. 1955. The past and present status of the Wryneck in the British Isles. *Bird Study* 10:112-132.

NEWTON, A. 1896. *A Dictionary of Birds*. A. & C. Black.

PETERSON, R.T., MOUNTFORT, G. & HOLLOM, P.A.D. 1956. *A Field Guide to the Birds of Britain and Europe*. Collins.

PRIESTLEY, M. 1937. *A Book of Birds*. Victor Gollancz.

SHARROCK, J.T.R. (Ed.) 1976. *The Atlas of Breeding Birds in Britain and Ireland*. T. & A.D. Poyser.

SNOW, D.W. 1958. *A Study of the Blackbird*. London.

SWAINSON, C. 1885. *Provincial Names and Folklore of British Birds*. Trubman & Co for the English Dialect Society.

SWANN, H.K. 1913. *A Dictionary of English and Folk-names of British Birds*. Witherby.

WHITE, GILBERT 1789. *The Natural History of Selborne*. Edited by E.M.Nicholson, 1929. Thornton Butterworth.

WHITE, T.H. 1938. *The Sword in the Stone*. Collins.

WITHERBY, H.F., JOURDAIN, F.C.R., TICEHURST, N.F. & TUCKER, B.W. 1938. *The Handbook of British Birds*. Vols. I-V Witherby.